מזל טוב!

May you merit to build an everlasting home on the foundations of Torah & mitzvos. May you illuminate your surroundings and everyone you are in contact with.

— Rabbi Shmuli & Rivky Friedman

By the grace of G-d

THE BAILA FRIEDMAN EDITION

THE EDIFICE

Dating, Marriage and an Everlasting Home

From the life and teachings of

The Rebbe
Rabbi Menachem Mendel Schneerson

of righteous memory

HASIDIC archives

Compiled and adapted by **Dovid Zaklikowski**

Illustrated by **Annita Soble**

For my wife
Chana Raizel
- Dovid

The Edifice © 2019 Hasidic Archives
www.HasidicArchives.com
HasidicArchives@gmail.com
Facebook.com/HasidicArchives

All rights reserved, including the right to
reproduce this book or portions thereof,
in any form, without prior permission,
in writing, from Hasidic Archives

ISBN

Hardcover 978-1-944875-06-0
Paperback 978-1-944875-10-7

Design and Layout by Chaya M. Kanner

Printed in China

In loving tribute to

Baila Friedman

of blessed memory

Loving mother and educator, who guided myriads of women in building everlasting edifices

―ঽ

By her children

Nochi and **Miriam**

and grandchildren

Naftoli, Baila and Moshe Goldshmid

The Rebbe, Rabbi Menachem Mendel Schneerson

Contents

Love & Dating — 9

What Is Love?	10
Atomic Energy	12
Dating for Fun	14
Toxic Love	15
Equation of Two	16

Wedding — 19

Felicitations	20
Joy of Marriage	22
Three Circles	25
Ring Giving	26
Monetary Reminder	27
Bringing Joy	28
The Edifice	30
Why Wait?	32
Foot or Heart?	33
Reciprocity Effect	34
Blessings Genesis	36
Dance!	39
The Bride's Voice	40

Children — 43

The Goal	44
Seeing the Unity	45
Patience Creator	46
Be Fruitful	47
The Childless Woman	50
Both Parents	52

Married Life — 55

Finding Good	56
Full Personhood	57
Wedding Never Ends	58
A Gift for Your Wife	60
Developing Sensitivity	68
Perfection	70
Relative Perfection	71
Consideration under Duress	74

Living Waters — 79

All-Encompassing	84
Total Immersion	85
Stepping Stones	86
Like a Newborn	90
The Channel for Blessing	91
Protective Garments	92
Greater Heights	94
The Outcome	95
Humility	97

Addendums

Finding a Soulmate	101
Wedding Anxiety	117
Build Mikvahs!	123

Sources — 142

Acknowledgements — 146

It is only when I am asked for advice that I offer it as I see it, to the best of my knowledge, in the best interests of the inquirer and those in their inner circle. My advice is not in any way binding. It is advice which, I believe, is for their benefit, materially and spiritually.

—The Rebbe, August 22, 1974

Love & Dating

What Is Love?

Chana Sharfstein's innocence was stripped away the moment she learned of her father's senseless, fatal beating by a thug on a dark Boston night in 1953. After his death, Chana, 22, struggled with the challenges life presented as she attempted to recover. Since her siblings were all married, she was at home alone with her mother, who suffered deeply from their devastating loss.

One night, Chana made the journey to Lubavitch World Headquarters to meet the Rebbe for a private audience. The Rebbe asked Chana about her interests, concerns, and future plans, and listened carefully to her responses. From that time onward, the Rebbe became a father figure in her life, someone to whom she could turn for comfort and advice.

Several months later, during an impromptu visit to New York, she met with the Rebbe again. Chana told the Rebbe that she had met several young men, but none had piqued her interest.

"Is there someone else you are interested in?" the Rebbe asked. Yes, she said, a student who was a popular Hasidic singer had impressed her, and she felt something for him.

The Rebbe chuckled. "He is not the right one for you. True love is not the way it is portrayed in romantic books. It isn't an overwhelming, blinding emotion. Novels do not depict real life. Fiction is just that – fiction – but real life is different."

Most of Chana's ideas about marriage had been drawn from novels, and she had been disappointed when the young men she met did not appear to be princes with whom she could live happily ever after.

The Rebbe continued:

Love is an emotion that increases in strength throughout life. It is sharing, caring, and respecting one another. The love that a young bride feels is only the beginning of real love. It is the process of building a life together, a family unit, a home, that creates love. It is in the small acts of daily life that love flourishes and grows. The love you feel after five or ten years of marriage is a gradual strengthening of the shared bond. Ultimately, a couple feels completely bonded, so that each partner can no longer visualize life without his or her mate.

ATOMIC ENERGY

The potential of male-female relationships is like atomic energy. When used in a positive and holy way, there is nothing more powerful and precious. When used recklessly, without sacred context, it can be the most destructive force in existence.

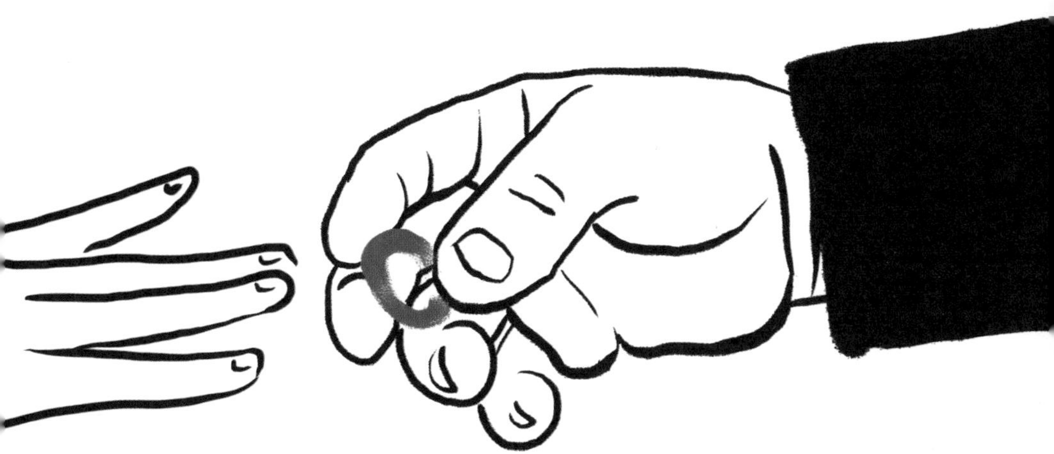

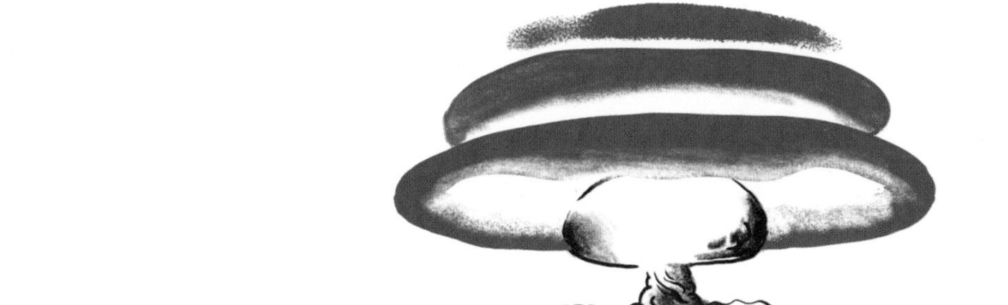

Dating for Fun

A relationship between a boy and girl should be only platonic. Often, however, these relationships grow deeper, but eventually end.

Dating without the goal of marriage detracts from the relationships the girl and boy will ultimately have with their respective spouses. Is it worth allowing the pleasure of dating for a few months or years to spoil what one hopes will last for many decades?

Toxic Love

It sometimes happens that there is a deep attraction between two people who should not be together, either for health reasons or because they are simply spiritually incompatible. It might be tempting to throw caution to the wind and pursue the relationship despite the obstacles, but it would not be wise. In fact, the deep feelings the couple has for each other should have the opposite effect. One would never willingly place a person one cared about in an environment that could be detrimental to their wellbeing.

EQUATION OF TWO

In marriage, one takes responsibility for another person's life. It follows that the best preparation for marriage is to develop and expand your . . .

. . . ability to give to others.

Wedding

*My Felicitations
to You . . .*

By the Grace of G-d
Greeting and blessing:

In reply to your letter in which you write about your forthcoming marriage, I am confident that both you and your chosen partner in life have firmly resolved to establish a truly Jewish home on the foundation of Torah and mitzvahs. In addition to the essential aspect of living up to the Jewish way of life, in accordance to G-d's will, this is also the channel to receive G-d's blessings and to ensure lasting happiness, materially and spiritually.

May G-d grant that your marriage take place in a happy and auspicious hour and be an "everlasting edifice."

With the blessing of *mazel tov*, *mazel tov*,

                M. Schneerson

Joy of Marriage

In the summer of 1950, Rabbi Leibel Posner proposed to his future wife, Thirza, and she happily accepted. Standing under the Williamsburg Bridge, the newly engaged couple dropped a few cents into a payphone and called the Rebbe's office to report the good news.

In the course of the conversation, the Rebbe asked Rabbi Posner, "When two people marry, what is the reason for the great joy that ensues?" Just as the cycle of life ends, people marry to create new life, the Rebbe said, acknowledging their own mortality. "If that is the case, why would it be such a joyous occasion?"

The cause for joy, the Rebbe explained:

In heaven, each soul is divided in two. One half is placed in a male body, the other in a female. At a wedding, we rejoice that the divided soul has been reunited.

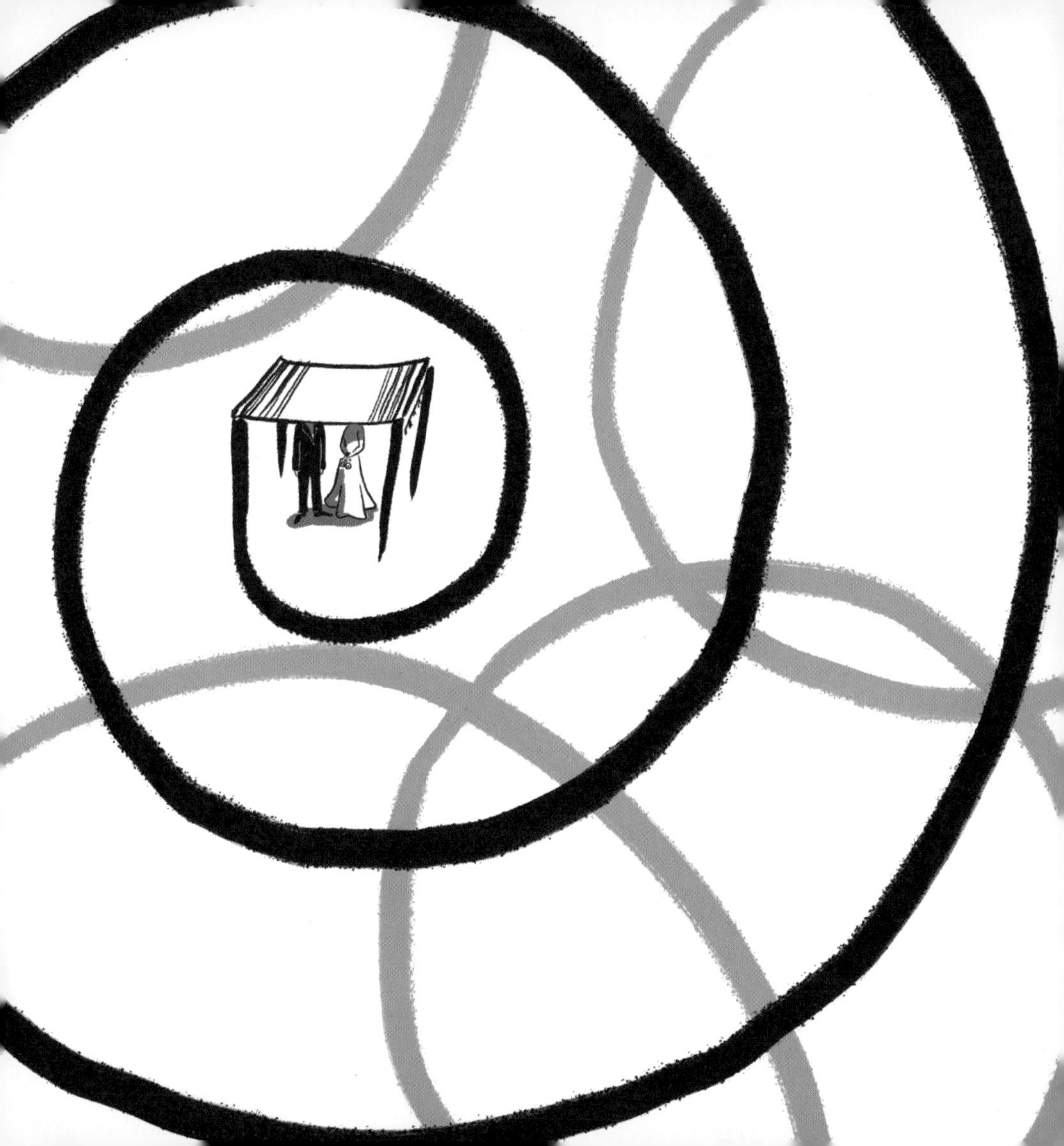

THREE CIRCLES

A Talmudic sage was once asked, "Since the creation of the world, what does G-d do?" The sage responded, "G-d spends time pairing men and women for marriage. Pairing soulmates is as difficult as splitting the Sea of Reeds." In order that the marriage should be sound there are three partners: the woman, the man, and G-d.

In kabbalah, G-d's presence is often represented by being encircled. Hence the encircling at a Jewish wedding of the three partners to bring a loftier level of spirituality in their marriage and be able to overcome the tribulations which unity could be fraught with: the bride circles the groom seven times, the groom places a circular wedding band on her finger, and the wedding canopy encircles and embraces them as they begin a new life together.

RING GIVING

Jewish tradition is that a man "acquire" his wife with the gift of a gold wedding ring which binds him to care for her and provide for her needs. This is not a literal acquisition, but rather a way to make the couple's commitment to each other and their new life together official and therefore more durable, as the verse says, "and they shall become one" (Genesis 2:25). The "transaction" ensures that the edifice they build is sound, strong, and not easily unraveled.

MONETARY REMINDER

Kesef, the Hebrew word for monetary value, can also be read as *koisef*, "yearning." This is the deeper significance of *kiddushin*, the part of the wedding ceremony when the groom sanctifies his bride by placing a ring on her finger. What seems like a financial transaction is actually the man's expression of love and yearning for the other half of his soul.

Bringing Joy

Fraida Jacobson was expecting her third child when she and her husband, Simon, fled the Soviet Union in 1947. Simon had been tortured by Communist agents and exiled to Siberia for his work in Chabad's system of underground schools.

To their great joy, their son Sholom was born in freedom in a displaced persons camp in Germany. The family later moved to France and, in 1952, to Toronto, Canada. Tragically, not long after, Simon passed away due to complications from the torture in Soviet prison. Fraida died a year later, leaving Sholom, seven, and his two brothers orphans.

Sholom joined his two brothers in New York, where he studied at the Chabad day school and lived with a local family. There he grew into a studious scholar, eventually joining a group of students who prepared the Rebbe's talks for publication.

In 1972, he became engaged to Faigel Springer. The wedding was to be celebrated in Israel, but as preparations moved forward, Sholom couldn't help being keenly aware of his parents' absence. After all, he would be standing under the wedding canopy alone.

The Rebbe understood Sholom's feelings, and, in appreciation for his work publishing the talks, took it upon himself to ease the pain, if only slightly. He asked one of Sholom's colleagues to travel to the wedding at his (the Rebbe's) expense. "Go into the office, and they will pay for the cost of the ticket."

The Rebbe also arranged for a respected Chabad disciple who was involved in publishing the Rebbe's talks in Israel to attend the wedding. Since Sholom and the disciple both worked in the same field, the Rebbe said, "This joyous occasion is his." The elderly man attended the wedding from beginning to end, dancing as if the groom were his own son.

In addition, the Rebbe asked Chabad in Israel to organize a surprise feast in the new couple's honor.

THE EDIFICE

At a Jewish wedding, we bless the couple that their home be "an everlasting edifice." This is not a poetic expression but a literal prescription for success. Just as a physical structure requires a solid foundation, a marriage must be founded on eternal Jewish tradition, teachings, and observance if it is to withstand the test of time.

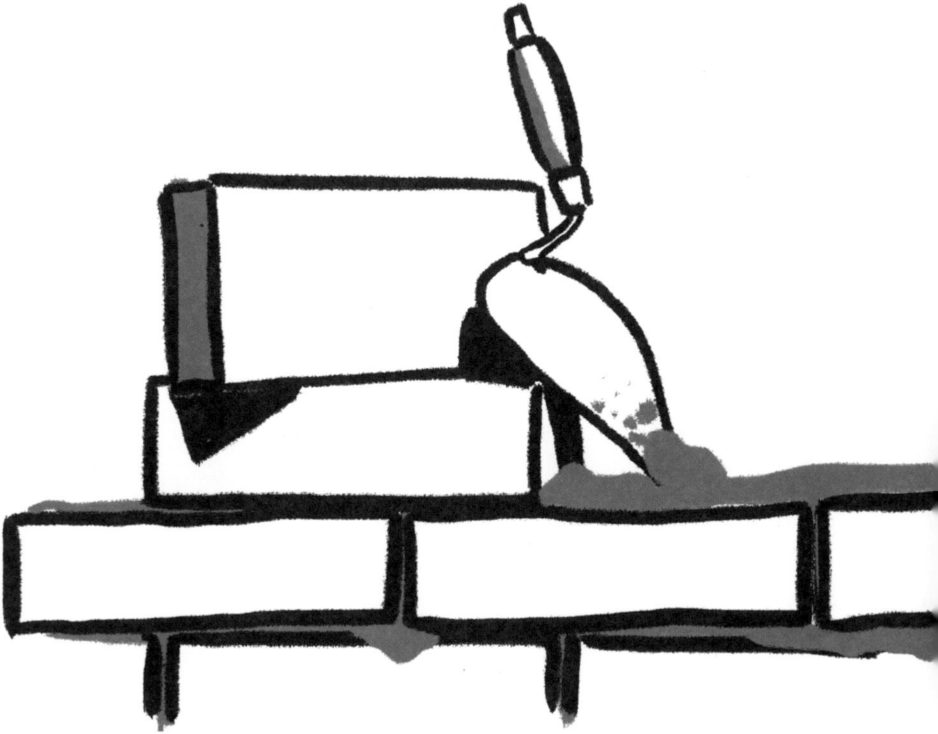

Why Wait?

She was American; he was Israeli. They met in New York, fell in love, and became engaged. The groom had a weekly Torah study session with Rabbi Dudi Goldschmidt, a Chabad representative in New York City, who suggested they visit the Rebbe for a blessing.

Standing in the Rebbe's office, they asked for a blessing for their wedding which was to be held in Israel in July, some five months from then.

"In July?" the Rebbe asked, "Why would you postpone a good thing for such a long time?"

The bride answered that the entire family would be in Israel then to commemorate the anniversary of passing of her brother, who had volunteered with the Israeli Defense Force during the 1982 Operation Peace for Galilee. "We want the wedding to be around the same time."

The Rebbe reiterated, "If it is something good, why wait so long?"

If it were held earlier, she replied, her parents would have to travel to Israel twice. "They do not have the time."

"If you find the time to get married, your parents will find the time to come to the wedding," the Rebbe answered simply.

That night, the engaged couple began to study the area of Jewish law related to married life, and a few weeks later, they had a Jewish marriage ceremony in New York.

Foot or Heart?

Yehudah Clapman loved Jewish customs. He loved them for their diversity and for what they represented, an unbroken chain of tradition passed from one generation of Jews to another. The Chabad community has their own customs, but Yehudah felt it couldn't hurt to add something new occasionally. When he found a custom he liked, he would consult the Rebbe about whether or not to adopt it.

Before Yehudah's wedding, he learned of an ancient remedy (*segulah*) stating that the spouse who steps on the foot of the other first under the wedding canopy will be dominant in the marriage. During a private audience, he asked the Rebbe if this was something he should do at his own wedding.

He told the young groom that stepping on his bride's foot in public would not be modest, and added that the idea behind the custom was flawed. Aggressive behavior would not bring submission from a spouse.

"If you will be the husband you are supposed to be, then your wife will listen to you."

RECIPROCITY EFFECT

Giving charity causes a reciprocal response from G-d: He becomes charitable to us. It follows that on the day of the wedding, when all of G-d's blessings are needed, it is proper for the future couple, the parents, the grandparents, and the entire family to give additional charity.

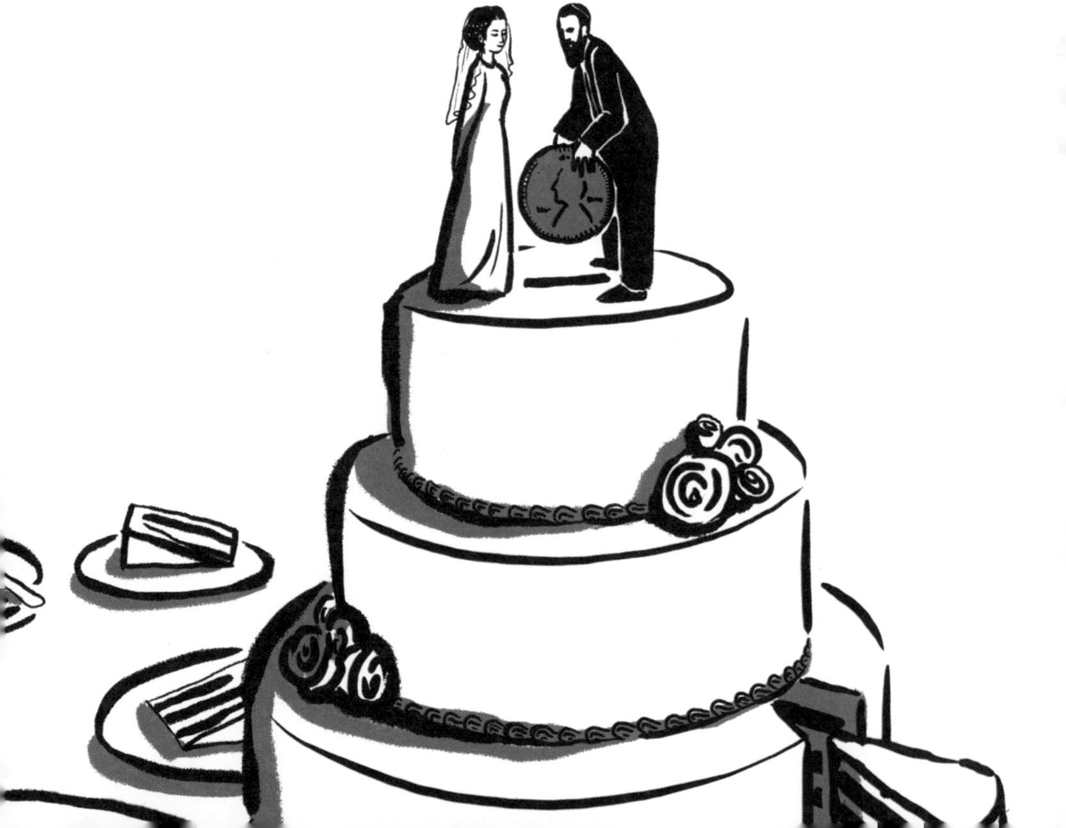

BLESSINGS GENESIS

After the ring is given and the marriage contract read, seven blessings, *sheva brachot*, are recited over a glass of wine from which the groom and bride both drink, concluding the ceremony. Several of the blessings, however, seem unrelated to the marriage ceremony itself. Why, then, do we recite them under the canopy?

The first blessing praises G-d who has "created all things for his glory." This is meant as a reminder to the couple that although they have come together on their own to build a home, the endeavor cannot succeed without G-d's blessing.

Similarly, the second blessing, "creator of man," reminds

the bride and groom that in having children of their own, they will be partnering with G-d, the original creator of all life. The third blessing elaborates: not only did G-d create man "in His image," He "prepared for him, from his own self, an everlasting edifice." The union of husband and wife is a divine creation, their ability to form an eternal "edifice," a family that will continue in perpetuity, a divine gift.

Finally, we acknowledge that even the joy we feel is a blessing on this momentous occasion. G-d does not want us to view marriage as a religious duty to be fulfilled in drudgery. Indeed, Adam and Eve's joy in each other in the Garden of Eden is taken as the ultimate expression of human happiness, "the sound of joy and the sound of happiness, the sound of the groom and the sound of the bride...."

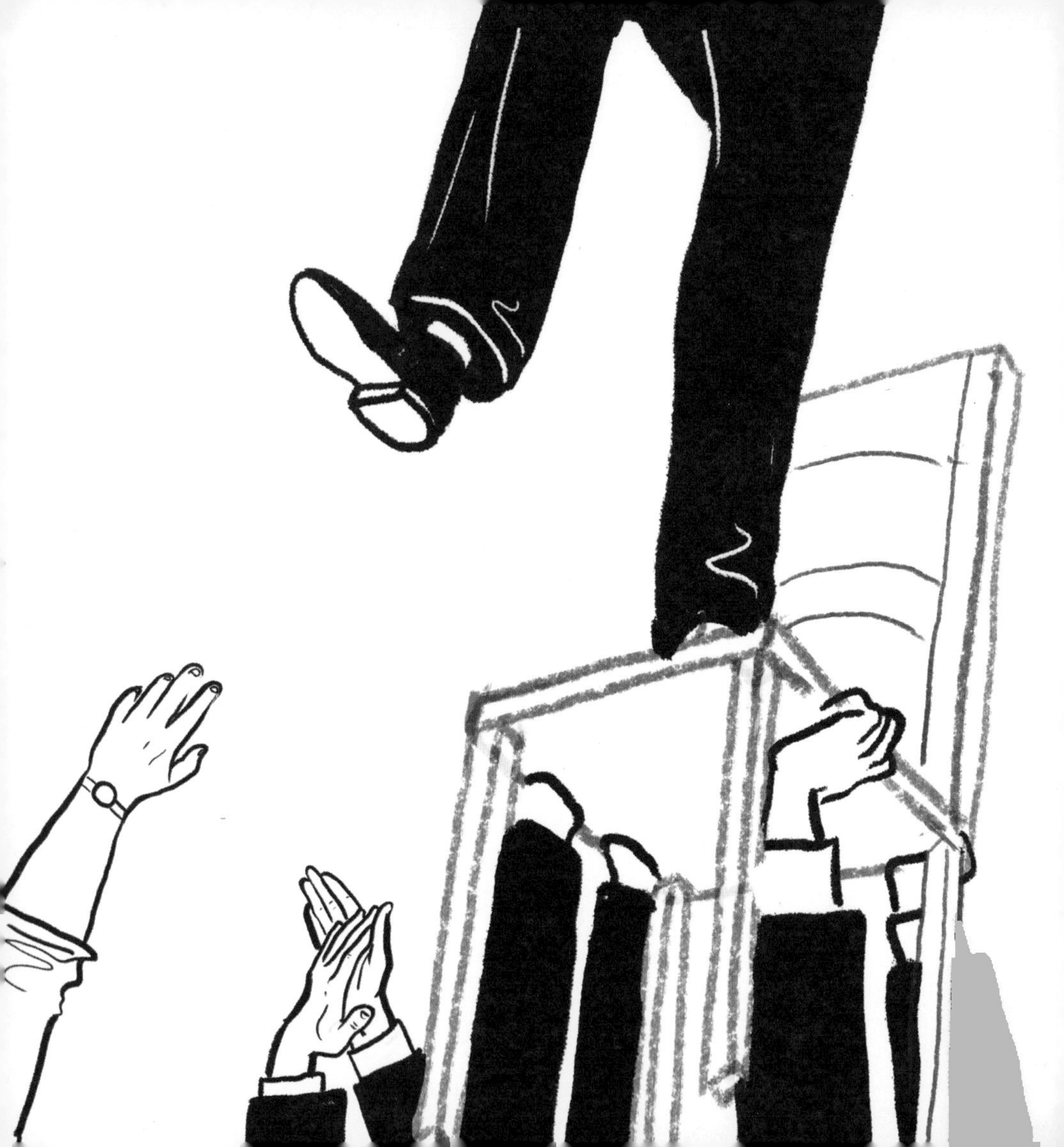

DANCE!

In kabbalah, walking symbolizes the normal way of journeying through life. Dancing is a break from the ordinary, a supernatural leap toward greater spiritual heights. Marriage, which brings the divine presence to rest in the union of husband and wife, is such a leap. That's why we dance at a wedding.

The Bride's Voice

The Rebbe received a large quantity of letters each day in many different languages, and he responded personally to each one. One of his aides, Dr. Nissan Mindel, was tasked with managing his English letters. Two or three times a week, he would spend six hours in the Rebbe's office taking dictation.

The Rebbe worked quickly, responding to one letter and reading another at the same time. Dr. Mindel, however, spent the rest of the week transcribing his notes and composing responses, which the Rebbe reviewed and edited.

It was unusual for the Rebbe to ask personal questions of his aide during work hours, but one day, during the week after Dr. Mindel's daughter's wedding, he made an exception.

For seven days after a wedding, the bride and groom are honored each night with a festive meal, at which the *sheva brachot*, the seven blessings said under the wedding canopy, are recited again. "Tell me," asked the Rebbe, "does the groom say words of Torah at the [*sheva brachot*] meal?"

Yes, Dr. Mindel replied. The groom had recited a Hasidic discourse from memory each evening.

Referring to the last of the seven blessings, "Let there speedily be heard in the cities of Judah . . . the sound of a groom and the sound of a bride," the Rebbe asked, "Last night you heard the sound of the groom. When will you hear the sound of the bride?"

Dr. Mindel relayed the message, and that night, the bride delivered some words of Torah at the celebratory feast.

Children

THE GOAL

The goal of marriage is the revelation of G-d's presence in our world. The revelation may take many forms, but the most obvious is the creation of new life, children.

SEEING THE UNITY

Where does the unification of
souls between man and wife
find its ultimate expression?
In the birth of a child.

Patience Creator

In 1957, four days before her wedding, Eileen Weiss, accompanied by her fiancé, met the Rebbe for the first time. Immediately, she was struck by the Rebbe's calming blue eyes. "They were unbelievable, the most beautiful things that I ever saw." In his presence, she felt her heart opening. "I was able to reveal certain things."

Eileen had grown up with one parent who was overbearing and struggled with impatience and anger. Now on the verge of starting her own family, she felt paralyzed with fear that she would follow in that parent's footsteps. She turned to the Rebbe and asked if she could speak to him alone. The Rebbe motioned for her groom to leave the room.

As soon as he left, Eileen broke down in tears. "I don't want to get married. If I get married, I will have a terrible temper, and my husband will surely want to divorce me. It is better to not have a wedding at all than to get married and then divorce."

The Rebbe reassured her that there was no need to cancel the wedding. G-d willing, she would have many children who would teach her to be patient. "Over time, the issue of impatience will get better." He advised her that until she had her first child, she should volunteer in the children's ward at a hospital.

When the groom reentered the room, the Rebbe gave them

blessings for their wedding and, uncharacteristically, escorted them to the door.

After her marriage, Eileen recalled, she did find herself struggling with impatience. "I was lucky that I realized I would have a problem with the anger. I worked on it and learned how to deal with the temptations."

Be Fruitful

After his father's passing in 1979, Rabbi Avrohom Yaakov Friedman ascended to the leadership of the Sadigura Hasidic dynasty, based in Israel. One of the issues on his mind at the time was the slow population growth in Israel, which the government seemed to be encouraging by actively promoting family planning.

Eager to discuss the problem, Rabbi Friedman came to visit the Rebbe on June 18, 1980. Part of the difficulty, he told the Rebbe, was social stigma. "The doctors make a mockery of families who have many children." It seemed ironic that the Israeli government was willing to spend thousands of dollars on each immigrant, yet actively discouraged its citizens from having more than a few children.

"The government needs to be encouraged to give a greater allowance for each child that is born," the Rebbe replied. This allowance should be given to all segments of the society and religions. "They are also commanded [to have children]," the Rebbe said, quoting the verse (Isaiah 45:18): "For so said the L-rd, the Creator of heaven . . . Who formed the earth and made it . . . did not create it for a waste. He formed it to be inhabited."

Taken aback, Rabbi Friedman asked why the Israeli government should encourage non-Jews to have children.

It is the Jews' responsibility, the Rebbe said, to make sure that non-Jews are aware of and fulfilled their Torah obligations. By discouraging births, the government was discouraging them from fulfilling the G-d-given command of, "He formed it to be inhabited."

It is difficult to find virtue in waiting to have children for financial reasons. Children are G-d's great and precious blessing. Would you tell someone who is giving you a coveted and priceless gift, "I do not want your gift now, but when I do, I will let you know"?

The Childless Woman

In 1977, Donna Halper was a radio announcer and host at WRVR Jazz in New York. Intuitive, curious, and a vivacious conversationalist, she was acquainted with many celebrities, so when she developed an interest in her Jewish roots, she didn't hesitate to reach out to the most prominent Jewish leader she could find. She wrote to the Rebbe with several questions that were bothering her.

"Does a woman who cannot have children have a place in Jewish life?" she asked. She knew that the Rebbe and his wife did not have children, and she wondered about the stigma that is often associated with childlessness in Orthodox communities.

To her surprise, the Rebbe responded with a three-page letter in which he answered her questions in great detail. Regarding infertility, the Rebbe wrote (contracted and adapted):

When a person, for some reason, is unable to perform a certain divine precept, there is a biblical ruling: "The Merciful One excuses a person who is incapable of performing his, or her, duty." Indeed, G-d, Who knows what is in everyone's heart, knows that were the person able, they would have performed it, and considers the thought in place of the deed.

Incidentally, it is noteworthy that of the various divine names, it is the name "Merciful One" that is used in the above ruling. This emphasizes that all G-d's precepts derive from His attribute of mercy and loving-kindness, which, like all divine attributes, is infinite. It follows that a person who is precluded from performing a precept by circumstances beyond his or her control is completely excused and exonerated.

Both Parents

In the early 1970s, *Hadassah Magazine*, the bi-monthly publication of the Hadassah Women's Zionist Organization, asked *The New York Times* columnist Ari Goldman to write about the role that fathers play in modern-day parenting.

As part of his research, Ari called Rabbi Yehudah Krinsky, a longtime aide to the Rebbe and the public relations director at Chabad headquarters, to ask what Chabad's approach to the subject might be. Rabbi Krinsky told him that the Rebbe had compiled a calendar of sayings and lessons drawn from Chabad teachings, which included the maxim of the fifth Chabad Rebbe, Rabbi Sholom Dovber Schneersohn, that a parent should spend at least half an hour every day thinking about the education of his children:

> *Rabbi Sholom Dovber once declared at a Hasidic gathering in 1904: "Just as putting on tefillin every day is a biblical commandment incumbent on every Jew, regardless of whether they are a great Torah scholar or a simple person, so too, it is an absolute obligation for every Jew to dedicate half an hour every day to contemplating their children's education, and to do everything in their power, and indeed, more than what is in their power, to see to it that they follow the path in which they are being guided."*

The journalist was impressed, though he apparently misunderstood the quotation and assumed that it represented a recent change in the traditionally sexist approach that Hasidim took to these matters. In fact, the saying was over seven decades old, and the calendar itself had been published in the 1940s:

> *Even in Hasidic homes, where the letter of Jewish law is strictly adhered to, there is a growing tendency for men to be involved with their children. In a popular calendar put out by the Lubavitcher Hasidim, there is the following quotation from the grand rabbi, Menachem M. Schneerson: "Just as it is a mitzva to put on tefillin every day, it is a mitzva for the father to be involved with the children every day."*

Rabbi Krinsky brought the published article to the Rebbe. Obviously disturbed by the implication that Judaism regards women as second-class citizens, the Rebbe took out a volume of Jewish law, based on the Talmud taught thousands of years earlier, turned to the laws of deceit, and told the aide that it was important that Jewish women know that Judaism holds them in high esteem:

> *A man should always be careful with respecting his wife, for the blessing in the home is only for his wife. This is what the sages told to their generation (Talmud, Baba Mezia 59a): To become wealthy, respect your wives.*

Married Life

Finding Good

The Jewish engagement contract states, "When you found a woman, you found good." In the woman's merit, the home is blessed with spiritual and material wealth.

Full Personhood

The sages tell us that without a spouse, one is not a "person" (Talmud, Yevamot 63a), as we read in Genesis (5:2), "Male and female He created them," and only then did he call the male "man." Man was not created to live only for himself, but to partner with a spouse and build a home in which to nurture children who will live on after him.

WEDDING NEVER ENDS

Man and woman are opposites — they cannot remain united without constant help from a higher power. It follows that one must "get married" anew each day, tapping into the spiritual energy of the wedding day to renew and strengthen the bond with one's spouse.

This should be done with the same joy that was felt under the wedding canopy.

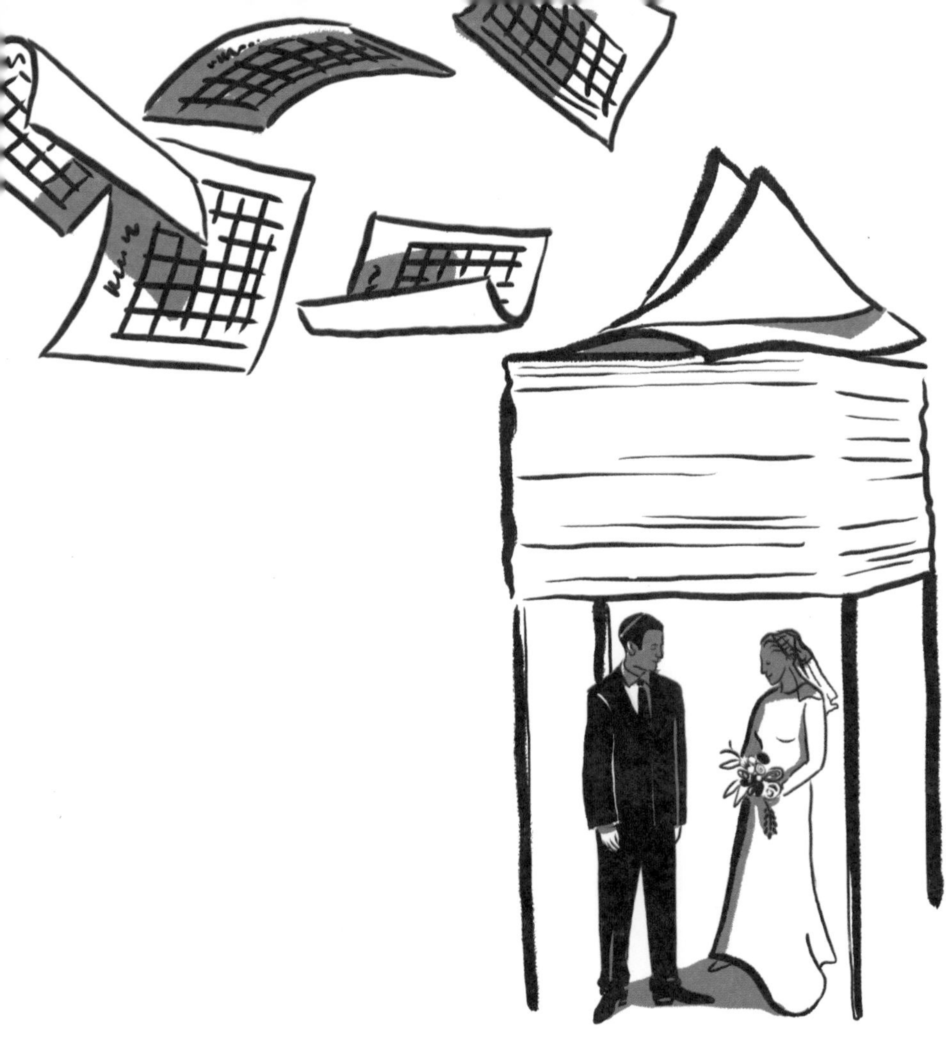

A Gift for Your Wife

It was a long trip from Australia to New York in the 1970s, but Rabbi Yitzchak Dovid Groner never complained. His yearly visit to the Rebbe's court was a treat, a chance to recharge his spiritual batteries for the challenging work of building Jewish life in Melbourne. His visits were usually scheduled during the Australian summer vacation, New York's winter months.

To the Rebbe, Rabbi Groner's trips were an opportunity to touch the remote Jewish communities that lay in his path. Before each visit, Rabbi Groner received detailed instructions about where he should stop and what he should do there. Thailand, the Philippines, China, and New Zealand all made appearances on his itinerary.

The Rebbe was eager for news of these isolated communities, where a visit from the Rebbe's emissary was a major event. "It is surprising to me that I have as yet received no report from your husband about the various cities and countries which he visited," the Rebbe wrote to Mrs. Groner in 1961. "However, inasmuch as the memory and impressions weaken with time, the time element is of importance.... I would like him to find every day a certain period to begin writing, without waiting until he can write the report fully all at once."

The extra stops added significantly to the length of Rabbi Groner's trips, and the Rebbe acknowledged that this required additional sacrifice of his wife, whose family and friends were far away in New York. The Rebbe encouraged her several times, praising her "pioneering spirit." The couple's mission, "to transform the whole of Jewish life in that remote continent," presented a unique "challenge and opportunity to the qualified person," he wrote.

The Rebbe also took a personal interest in Mrs. Groner's wellbeing. During a visit to New York for her son's wedding in 1972, she was standing on Eastern Parkway and saw the Rebbe approaching on foot from a distance. She felt that she was not ready to meet the Rebbe at that moment and turned away, giving enough time for the Rebbe to pass.

When she turned back, however, the Rebbe was standing there waiting for her to turn around. He asked her how she was and if everything was okay, then continued on his way.

The summer before, in 1971, Rabbi Groner had been in New York, while Mrs. Groner stayed home. The Rebbe gave him a mission to visit England, India, Iran, Israel, Italy, and Singapore on his way back to Australia, and before he left, the Rebbe called him to his office and gave him twenty-six ten-dollar bills.

Since his wife had not accompanied him, the Rebbe said, one of the bills should be considered his contribution toward a gift for her. Rabbi Groner bought his wife an Indian sari, which she later used to make a dress for her son's wedding.

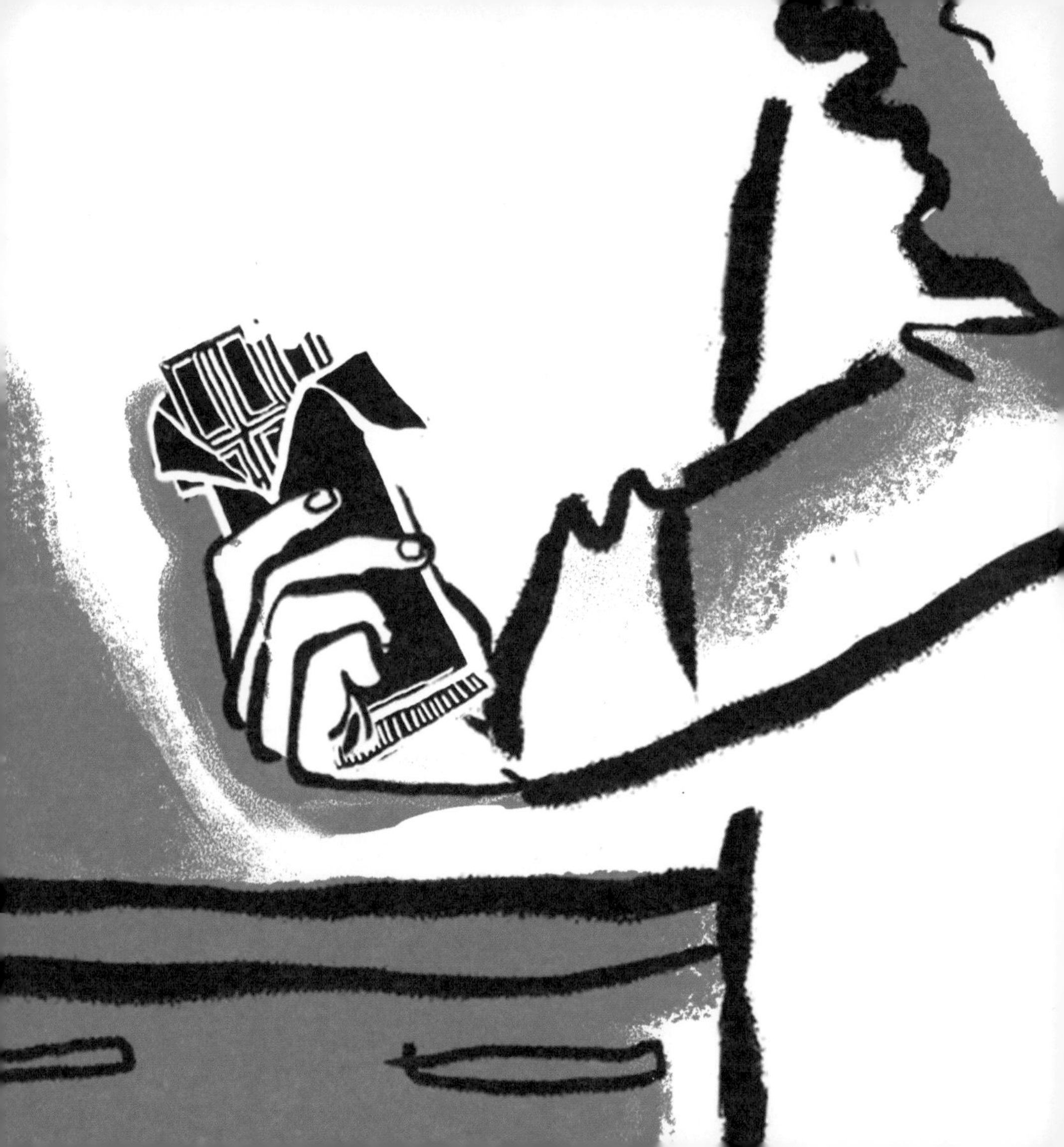

You conceal your faults from yourself and others, so do the same for your spouse.

Place their faults to the side and admire their virtues.

This is practical love.

Solomon said, "Just as water reflects an image of our face, so does one heart reflect another" (Proverbs 27:20). A loving attitude, kind disposition, and conciliatory feelings will evoke the same emotions in your spouse.

―§―

There are two basic paths in marriage: to focus on your spouse's negative qualities, or to look for the good. The latter path strengthens those good traits, benefiting both parties.

―§―

When it comes to longstanding, stable situations in which a spouse is comfortable, changing them will require more than an intellectual justification. You will need to appease him or her in other ways.

The mark of a good relationship is when you do something for your spouse because you desire to, not because you feel obligated.

Make an extra effort to give attention to your significant other. It can improve even their physical health.

Especially when there are children involved, who need the attention and love of both parents, a couple should do everything in their power to create a peaceful home and wholesome relationship.

Whom you marry is one of the most important decisions you will make in life. With infinite kindness, G-d provided Jewish observance and traditions for married life that are vessels for great blessings, as well as protection from undesirable situations.

Marriage is not about transforming or educating your partner. It is unrealistic to enter a marriage with that intention, and constant pressure to change from a spouse will eventually create resentment, and damage the relationship.

Peace in the home is a critical element in Jewish life. The morning prayers extol bringing peace between husband and wife as one of the few mitzvahs from which a person can benefit in this world and the next.

Indeed, marital accord is so precious to G-d that He commanded, "Erase My name for the sake of harmony in the home"

Talmud, Hullin 141a

Developing Sensitivity

Rabbi Shimon Lazaroff's parents displayed tremendous sacrifice to maintain Jewish tradition in the Soviet Union, despite Communist persecution. His father died by the hands of the Communists before he was born, and he was named after him. His mother raised him to be a fierce and fearless Jew. Rabbi Lazaroff immigrated to America in 1957, got married, and devoted himself to developing Jewish life in the country, organizing activities on college campuses and in small communities.

Once, during a private audience with the Rebbe, he handed the Rebbe a note with four questions about his activities, and a fifth, personal question. As a young fellow, he didn't understand that the final question, and any subsequent discussion, would have evoked his wife's discomfort. The Rebbe was sensitive to the fact, however, and responded to only the first four questions, ignoring the fifth. Rabbi Lazaroff wondered why, but did not ask.

The following day, the Rebbe's aide called the young rabbi to his office. "In regard to your fifth question, the Rebbe asked me to tell you his response...."

A short time later, when the young couple decided that they were ready to serve as Chabad-Lubavitch emissaries, they scheduled another audience with the Rebbe. Rabbi Lazaroff wrote a note requesting the Rebbe's blessing, which they both signed.

During the meeting, the Rebbe turned to Mrs. Lazaroff. "I see your signature here, but do you know what you signed?" She confirmed that she understood the contents of their letter.

"Did you sign the letter happily," the Rebbe pressed, "or because you felt compelled?" Mrs. Lazaroff said she was willing and glad to devote her life to serving a Jewish community.

Only once he had assured himself of her consent did the Rebbe give the couple his blessing to pursue their life's dream as Chabad representatives in Texas.

Perfection

Humans are imperfect; perfection belongs to G-d alone. Every person needs to make sacrifices and adjustments in marriage. This applies not just to your spouse, but to you too.

Relative Perfection

We all maintain strengths in specific areas, so "perfection" is relative when it comes to spouses. Still, G-d advises us to go "from strength to strength" (Psalms 84:8), indicating that everyone needs to grow continuously.

Many people endure difficulties in their marriages and overcome them. The real problem is when there is a lack of will to correct the situation. In such cases, a competent mentor or psychologist should be consulted, and the greatest effort made to amend, for our sages have said, "Between husband and wife the divine presence rests."

Even if you are (almost) completely right and your spouse is (almost) completely wrong, it is still incumbent upon both parties to do everything in their power to see the other's viewpoint and achieve harmony.

Marital arguments can become very heated, making it difficult, if not impossible, to hold a levelheaded conversation. In such cases, consult with a discreet and objective third party. This person can be a mutual friend, professional, or rabbi with experience in this field.

To successfully repair a marriage, the approach should be that all the problems can be fixed. It is best not to acknowledge the possibility of divorce.

Once a couple has been blessed by G-d with children, maintaining a stable and peaceful home becomes of the utmost importance. After all, it is the parents' responsibility to educated them and escort them to marriage. It's true that divorce is sometimes unavoidable, but it should be viewed as a tragedy, for both the couple and their children.

Consideration under Duress

The woman had endured many miscarriages and struggled with her health. Her husband, a Holocaust survivor, tried to acclimate to his new life with no family support in a country where he did not speak the language. As if that were not enough, several of their children were gravely ill.

The Rebbe encouraged the couple through their difficulties, reminding them to place their faith in G-d:

> *A Jewish person should put his or her faith only in G-d, the Creator and Master of the world, Who guides all its destinies, and Who is the healer of the sick and the source of all good.*

> *Because G-d is good, He wants everybody, and Jews especially, to be happy. It happens, however, that we, with our fleshy eyes, cannot see and understand His ways. But we must be firm in our faith that only good can come from the good G-d, and that the good will become apparent eventually.*

With his wife unable to work, the man took responsibility for supporting his family. His job was demanding, and though he tried to help at home, his wife felt that he did not do enough.

In private audiences and letters, the Rebbe encouraged the man to try harder. "I once again emphasize that you need to make a great effort, in the most fitting way possible, not to hinder, G-d forbid, the marital harmony in your home," he wrote on one occasion.

The woman wrote frequently to the Rebbe, describing her travails and expressing her frustration with her husband, who, it seemed to her, was more devoted to his job than to his family. At the time, only the wife read English, and the Rebbe made a point of writing back to her in English, in case her husband inadvertently opened one of the letters. Both of them, he wrote, needed to be more considerate:

This is in reply to your letter in which you write about the relationship between you and your husband. I trust that there has already been an improvement, or at least that one is on its way....

Any job generates a certain amount of nervous tension, and more so when he takes his job and duty seriously. Therefore patience and consideration on your part would do a great deal to improve the relationship and bring about the desired harmony and peace, which, as you know, is the "vessel" in which G-d's blessings are contained....

To someone who wrote about financial loss:

I already cautioned you several times about marital harmony. What can I do if you do not heed at all? Instead, you continue to stubbornly follow your emotions.

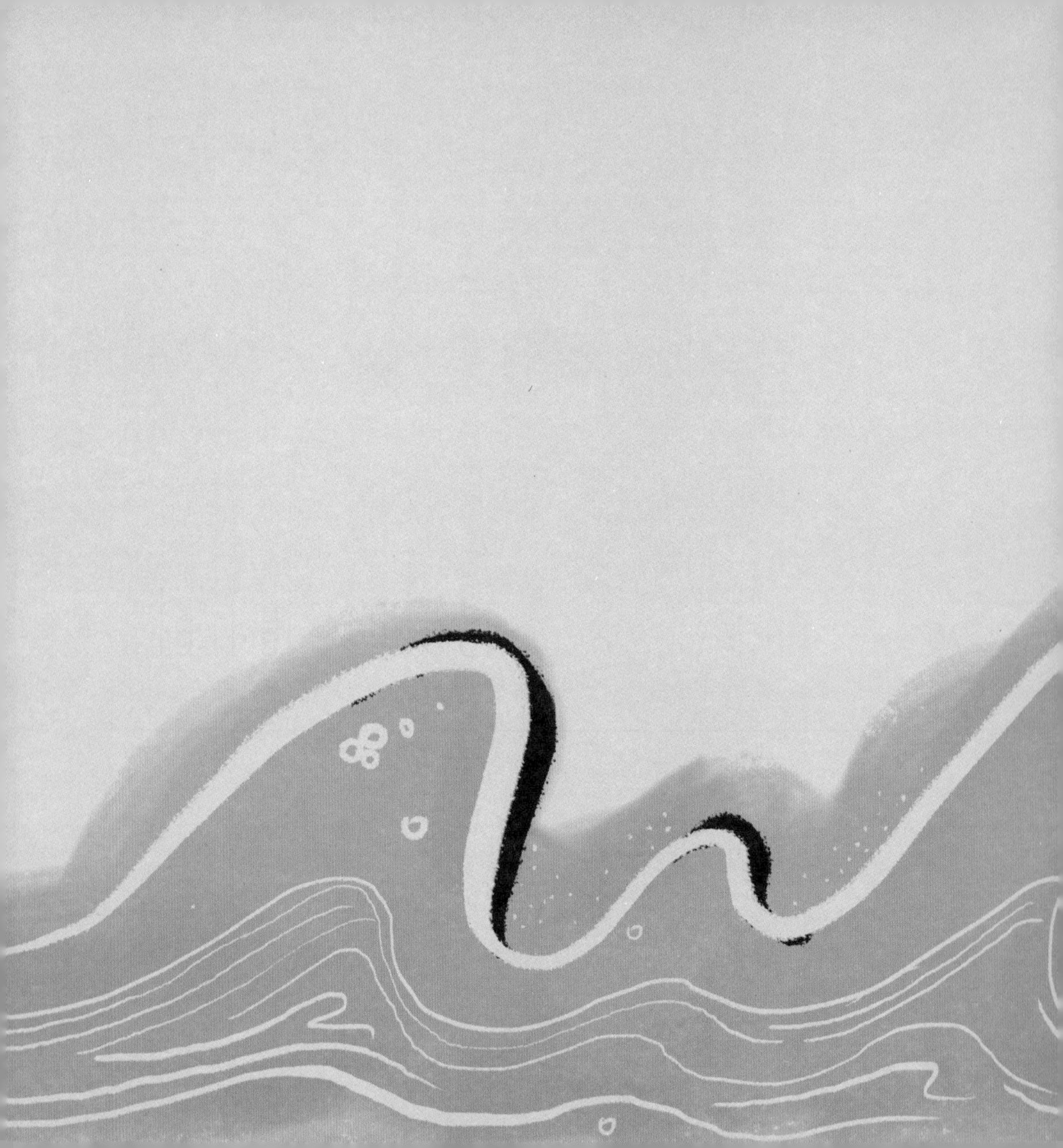

Living Waters

*Adapted from the
teachings of Chabad*

To the uninitiated, a modern-day mikvah looks like a miniature swimming pool. Its ordinary appearance, however, belies its primary place in Jewish life and law. The mikvah offers the individual, the community, and the nation of Israel the remarkable gift of purity and holiness. No other religious establishment, structure, or rite can affect the Jew in this way and, indeed, on such an essential level. Its extraordinary power, however, is contingent on its construction in accordance with the numerous and complex specifications outlined in Jewish law.

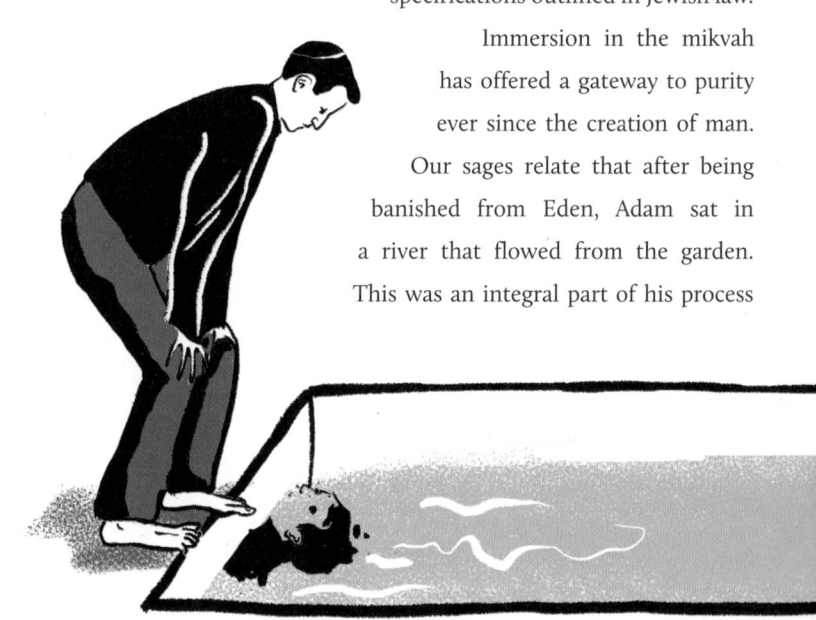

Immersion in the mikvah has offered a gateway to purity ever since the creation of man. Our sages relate that after being banished from Eden, Adam sat in a river that flowed from the garden. This was an integral part of his process of return to G-d, of his attempt to return to his original perfection.

Before the revelation at Sinai, all Jews were commanded to immerse themselves in preparation for coming face-to-face with G-d.

As the Jews travelled in the desert toward the Land of Israel, the famed "well of Miriam" served as a mikvah. And Aaron and his sons' induction into the priesthood was marked by immersion in the mikvah.

In Temple times, the priests, as well as each Jew who wished entry into the House of G-d, had to immerse in a mikvah.

The primary uses of mikvah today are

delineated in Jewish law and date back to the dawn of Jewish history. They cover many elements of Jewish life. Mikvah is an integral part of conversion to Judaism.

Mikvahs are used, this is less widely known, for the immersion of new pots, dishes, and utensils before they are used by a Jew. The mikvah concept is also the focal point of the *taharah*, the purification rite of a Jew before they are laid to rest and the soul ascends on high. The manual pouring of water in a highly specific manner over the entire body of the deceased serves this purpose.

Mikvah is also used by men on various occasions; with the exception of conversion, they are all customary. The most widely practiced are immersion by a groom on his wedding day and by every man before Yom Kippur. Many Hasidic men use the mikvah before each Shabbat and holiday, some even making use of mikvah each day before the morning prayers. But the most important and general usage of mikvah is for purification by the menstruant woman.

For the menstruant woman, immersion in a mikvah is part of a larger framework best known as *taharat hamishpachah*, or family purity, a system predicated on the woman's monthly cycle. Immersion in the mikvah is the culmination of this discipline. It is a special moment for the woman who has adhered to the many nuances of the mitzvah and has anticipated this night.

In this section we explore mikvah through the teachings of the Rebbe and his predecessors. When all is said and done, however, we will never understand the ultimate reason for the framework of family purity and its culmination – the mitzvah of mikvah. We observe simply because G-d ordained it. Still, these insights can add dimension and meaning to our mikvah experience.

ALL-ENCOMPASSING

Immersion in the mikvah waters symbolizes the all-encompassing G-dliness in our world. When you immerse in the mikvah, you submerge your understanding of this world and connect yourself to the higher reality: the G-dliness that is the essence of our daily life and all our surroundings.

TOTAL IMMERSION

The amount of water in a mikvah must be at least enough to encompass the entire body (in the measurement of Talmudic times, 40 *seah*, over 87 gallons). The letters of the Hebrew word for immersion (*tvilah*), may be rearranged to form the Hebrew word for spiritual nullification (*bittul*) before G-d. Nullification creates space within a person, which becomes a vessel for G-dliness. This is the meaning of Maimonides' statement that immersing in the mikvah is submerging "the soul in the waters of knowledge."

STEPPING STONES

The need for a person to purify themselves by immersing in a mikvah implies that something is amiss spiritually. But a state of impurity is not necessarily a negative thing. In describing the Israelites' encampments in the desert after the exodus from Egypt, the Torah uses the word "travels" (Exodus 40:36) rather than "stops." For even our pauses – our spiritual low points – are part of our journey of spiritual growth.

These stops,
the Torah teaches us, are
stepping stones to greater heights.

Menstruation represents the loss of a potential life. This absence of life creates a space which has the potential to be filled by something unholy. But only in a woman can there be that exalted possibility – a partnership with the Creator in producing a new life. When the menstrual cycle ends and the woman counts the seven "clean days," the possibility for life is reborn. And upon immersing in the mikvah she ascends into holiness.

We have seven character traits: loving-kindness, discipline, compassion, endurance, humility, bonding, and sovereignty. A woman counts seven days from the end of her menstrual cycle and refines these seven character traits by finding ways to use them for good deeds and holy acts.

Blood symbolizes passion. When the body naturally removes blood, it is because there is the possibility for passion to be channeled in the wrong direction. In order to recognize that possibility and distance oneself from it, one needs to immerse in water and focus one's passion on good and G-dly pursuits.

The body naturally removes menstrual blood – which symbolizes passion that might be channeled incorrectly – because a person in essence is good. The body wants to use its passion to fulfill the purpose for which it was created: to make a dwelling place for G-d in this world.

When a woman goes to the mikvah, the potential for new life within her and future generations that will follow immerse with her. This mitzvah influences the marital happiness of the couple and affects the character of their offspring.

Like a Newborn

In the 1960s, a Brooklyn woman was considering converting to Judaism. She contacted a rabbi who informed her of the requirements, one of which is immersion in a mikvah. She was ready to do everything except for the immersion, which she found difficult to comprehend. The rabbi advised her to go to the Rebbe with her dilemma.

The Rebbe explained to her in a private audience: According to the Talmud, a person who undergoes conversion is considered a newborn. When an embryo forms in the mother's womb, it is in a placenta surrounded by water. Similarly, the convert immerses entirely in the waters of the mikvah and emerges a newborn person.

Every person has a pure soul at birth. During life one may do things which have a negative impact on the soul. Immersion in the mikvah is a form of rebirth, and through it a person returns to the original state of purity.

The Channel for Blessing

All Elizabeth Applebaum wanted was a child.

When the journalist got married at the age of 30 in 1989, she made a point of observing the laws of family purity, immersing in the mikvah each month. But though she prayed fervently for a child, month after month pregnancy tests were negative.

A friend suggested that she write to the Rebbe asking for a blessing. She did, but did not get a response.

A short while later she received a diagnosis of endometriosis, and her doctor suggested she have surgery to correct it. "Everything looks fine now," Dr. Weinberg, the surgeon, told her. "The endometriosis likely accounts for your inability to get pregnant."

But the negative pregnancy tests continued. When Ms. Applebaum met her friend again, she described her frustration. "Why not just try to contact the Rebbe again?" the friend suggested.

Ms. Applebaum agreed to try again, and this time the Rebbe responded, urging her to carefully review the laws of family purity.

She didn't understand. Hadn't she been observing the laws scrupulously for more than two years?

"I was convinced that I already knew them so well," she said.

But she called her friend and made time to review some of the laws. To her astonishment, she discovered that she had been going to the mikvah a day early for the past two years.

She immediately corrected her calendar, and the very next month she was overjoyed to find that she was pregnant.

PROTECTIVE GARMENTS

Our good deeds, our daily actions in following G-d's directives, create positive, protective garments for our inner beings. When a husband and wife join together with G-d in purity to create a new life, they also create a positive and protective garment for the soul of the newborn, a garment that will continue to protect him or her into adulthood.

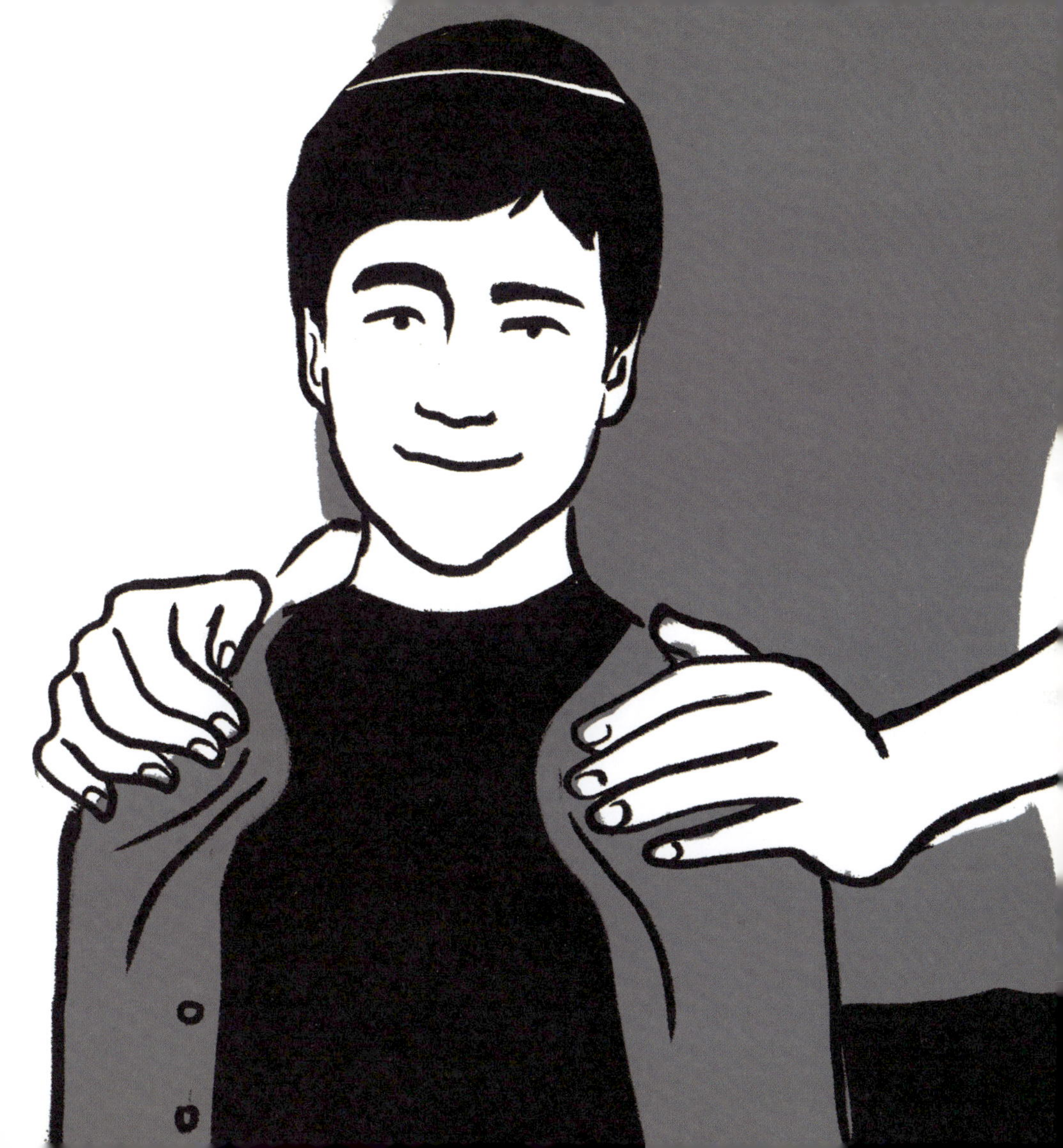

GREATER HEIGHTS

G-d created the world by contracting and concealing His infinite light. Traveling downward from one level to the next, through myriad spiritual worlds, this light is slowly concealed. All this is for what purpose? To create our world – where G-d is, at first glance, concealed. For were the G-dliness in our world to be openly revealed, it would be impossible not to fulfill His will. We reach the highest levels of G-dliness by serving our Creator here, in this world of darkness and concealment. So too, when one is in a state of so-called impurity, it is nothing but a concealment that will ultimately lead to greater revelation.

THE OUTCOME

Spiritual pursuits such as prayer, Torah study, and immersion in a mikvah are not for our personal refinement alone. Their primary purpose is to lead us to actions that make this world a better place. The fulfillment of the mitzvah of immersion occurs not while a woman is submerged in the mikvah, but once she surfaces. This teaches us that the purity of this mitzvah should find expression in all her future thought, speech, and action, for she is now a renewed person.

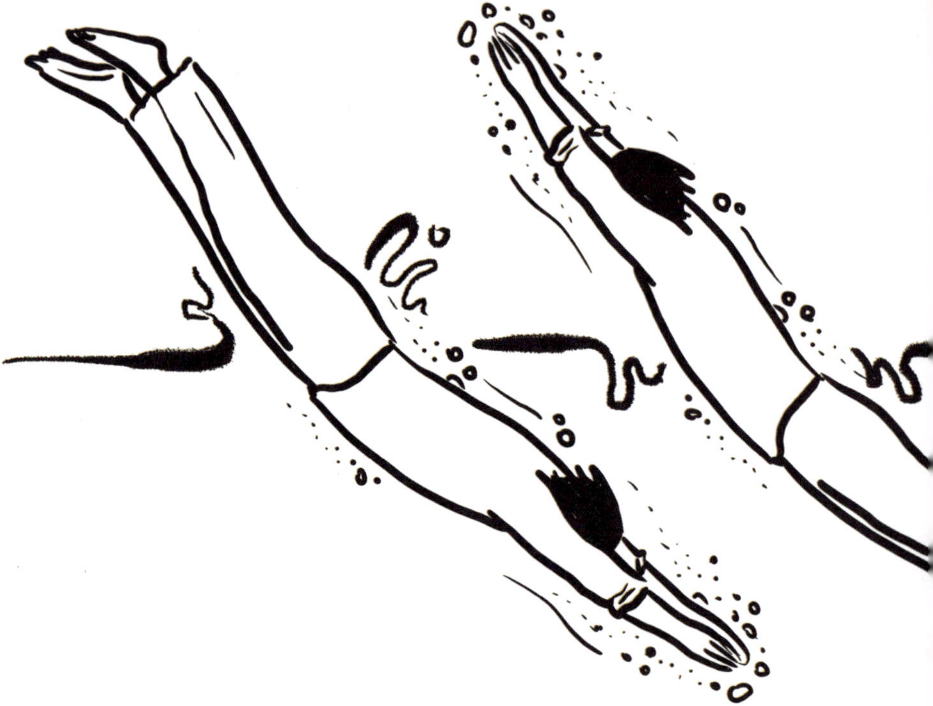

HUMILITY

As the mikvah waters envelope you, you recognize G-d's omnipresent sovereignty, and you become humble before the Creator. This brings you to greater spiritual heights, beyond understanding, a level known as G-d's crown. This level cannot be touched by sinful actions. There, you are connected with G-d alone, via your true essence.

Purity is a spiritual state that transcends the grasp of the human mind. It is one of the observances that G-d chose that we do not fully comprehend.

While we may know that immersing in the mikvah has benefits, fulfilling such commandments solely because they are G-d's will creates a deep connection with Him. These commandments bring us to a level that is beyond reason.

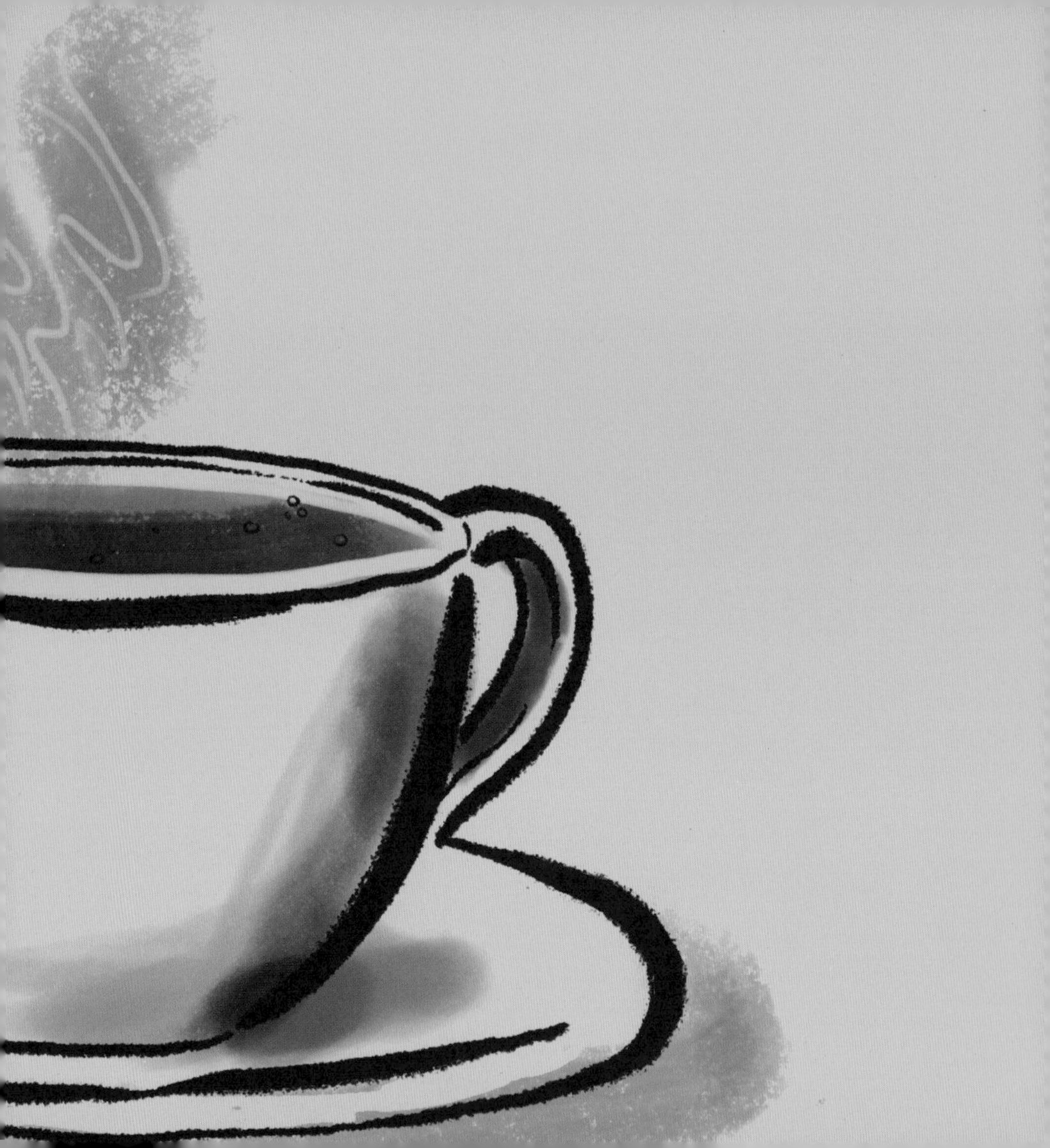

ADDENDUM I

FINDING A SOULMATE

THE SEARCH

The Talmudic sages state, "It is the duty of a man to seek out a woman." Leave your home and comfort zone, and search for your soulmate with the same intensity that you would search for an important lost object.

YOUR EFFORT

You have a soulmate. But finding your soulmate requires work. Don't expect them to be delivered on a silver platter. Your participation is critical.

More than Basic Love

A young man who lived in Israel had been suggested as a potential husband for 18-year-old Yehudis Fishman, but she wasn't sure it was a good idea. The couple who had proposed the match didn't know her well, she recalled, "nor what I wanted from life."

Still, she felt pressured to pursue the opportunity. She had written to the Rebbe for advice when she was younger, and her first impulse now was to consult him. In this case, she decided, a letter would not suffice. She took the bus to Lubavitch World Headquarters in Crown Heights, Brooklyn.

Once she got there, however, she realized that she had no hope of seeing the Rebbe without an appointment, usually made months in advance. She was so overwhelmed that she just sat outside the building, sobbing. An elderly gentleman, who she later found out was the Rebbe's senior aide, approached her and asked what was wrong. "I need to talk to the Rebbe," she said.

"Wait here a minute," he murmured. He returned a while later and said she had an appointment for the very next day.

Yehudis entered the Rebbe's study the next day with great trepidation. Her knees felt like jelly, and she had to hold on to the desk for support. "But as soon as I looked into the Rebbe's calm, clear, compassionate blue eyes, I relaxed a bit."

She explained her situation as concisely as she could. The Rebbe's response was immediate and definitive: "He is there in Israel and you are here. You are very different from each other. Remove him from your agenda."

"I walked out exhilarated," Yehudis said of that 1961 audience. "I felt I had found a guide, an advocate, and a friend. I was no longer alone in the world."

Sometime later, she dated a young businessman. But again, she was plagued by doubts about their compatibility. This time she made an appointment ahead of time through the Rebbe's office and traveled to Crown Heights on the appointed day.

After she explained her dilemma, the Rebbe asked in Yiddish, "Do you like this man?"

It was an obvious question, but coming from a rabbi, it took her by surprise. She gulped. "I have the basic love of a fellow Jew for him."

The Rebbe responded, again in Yiddish, "For a husband, one must have more than plain, basic love of a fellow Jew."

How can a dating couple differentiate true feelings of love from fleeting emotions that will pass with time? There are two ways: First, they could continue dating to allow more substantial feelings to develop. Second, they could completely separate for at least a week or more. If they miss or long for each other and want to meet again, it is more than a passing infatuation.

Do not hypothesize about what is going through the mind of the man you are dating. What he may or may not think is not relevant. If there is no direct rejection and you're still able to communicate, continue to acquaint yourselves.

Feelings matter. Even if your mind tells you that a person has all the qualities you desire, the lack of physical attraction is a serious issue that has to be considered before making a decision.

Who Are You Marrying?

Berel Futerfas' father had been exiled to Siberia for promoting Jewish observance in the Soviet Union; his mother was in England, and Berel himself was studying in New York. So when he reached marriageable age, Berel had to rely on more distant relatives to help find a suitable match.

His friend and cousin, the Chabad representative in Miami, Florida, suggested Naomi, a friend of his wife's, and Berel was delighted. He knew the rabbi shared his ethos of Chabad activism coupled with a fiery love for G-d and Jewish observance. Surely the girl would be a good match for him.

Their first date lasted several hours. As they spoke about their families, Naomi revealed that her father was the rabbi in a Conservative synagogue. Berel's initial good impression quickly transformed into disbelief. Could the son of a man who had given everything for Torah observance marry someone whose parents practiced a Judaism founded on compromise? It was inconceivable.

"Is this what my father sacrificed for?" he asked himself.

The date ended at midnight, and Berel went straight to Lubavitch World Headquarters, where the Rebbe was working late, as usual. He penned an emotional letter describing the situation and handed it to the Rebbe's aide.

"You are marrying the girl," the Rebbe responded. "Do not worry about who the parents are."

Who Wants Whom?

Determined to avoid the fate of their parents who were died at the hands of the Communists, Zalman and Shula Kazen fled the Soviet Union in 1946 with their young children and made their way to a displaced persons camp in Germany. Seven years later, with the assistance of the Hebrew Immigrant Aid Society (HIAS), they moved to the United States. HIAS arranged for an apartment in Cleveland, Ohio, but Shula wanted to live in New York, where the Rebbe and the majority of the Chabad community were located.

In a private audience with the couple, the Rebbe said, "Cleveland is also a nice place, with nice people and a good school." Turning to Zalman, he said, "In my opinion you should be a ritual slaughterer. Be a rabbi and lead the prayer services [on the Sabbath and holidays]."

Not long after they moved, the Rebbe instructed them to reach out to assimilated Jews in their area and encourage them to become more observant and to send their children to the Jewish school. So it was that the Kazens, the wounds of their own persecution still fresh, became the Rebbe's emissaries, imparting the passion for Judaism they had learned from their parents to the Jews of Cleveland.

"We were taught that Jewish continuity, the future of the Jewish people, depended on the kind of courage that the Rebbe exemplified. This is the kind of bravery and commitment we tried to emulate," Zalman said in 2005. By then the Kazens had been serving the Cleveland community for over five decades.

Even as a young girl, the Kazens' daughter Devorah took it for granted that her family was guided by the Rebbe in all of their major decisions. Like her parents, she trusted that whatever the Rebbe advised was for her benefit.

When it came time for her to marry, a list of names was drawn up and given to the Rebbe, who circled the name of a young man he thought would be an appropriate match. The couple would, of course, meet and get to know each other. Still, Devorah recalled "a wonderful feeling that this is what the Rebbe had in mind for me."

After meeting, the two decided to marry. In a private audience, Devorah asked the Rebbe for his blessing.

Acknowledging that the match had been his own suggestion, the Rebbe asked, "Do you want to marry him?"

"The Rebbe suggested this young man, and thus, for sure I want to marry him," Devorah replied.

"Do you want him?" the Rebbe asked again.

"The Rebbe suggested it. Of course I want to marry him."

The Rebbe became more serious, "Do you want him?"

Devorah realized that the Rebbe would not be satisfied until she expressed her own preference. "Yes, of course I want to marry him."

The Rebbe showered her with blessings, adding, "Bring [spiritual] light and warmth around you, and it will be light and warm in your home."

To one who was depressed because
she could not find a spouse:

Every day, in the morning, you say 18 blessings thanking G-d for your daily functions. This is a reminder to count your blessings before looking at what is missing. Thank G-d, you have been blessed with good health, good parents, an education, a positive atmosphere, a good job, etc.

Clearly you want to marry, but while many suitable names have been proposed, it seems there is a constant search for faults and excuses to say no. When that attitude changes, everything in this area will fall into place.

LIFETIME DECISION

Marriage needs to be consistent and stable. While dating, take into consideration the difficulties and challenges that life inevitably presents. Will the two of you be able to aid each other in your daily struggles?

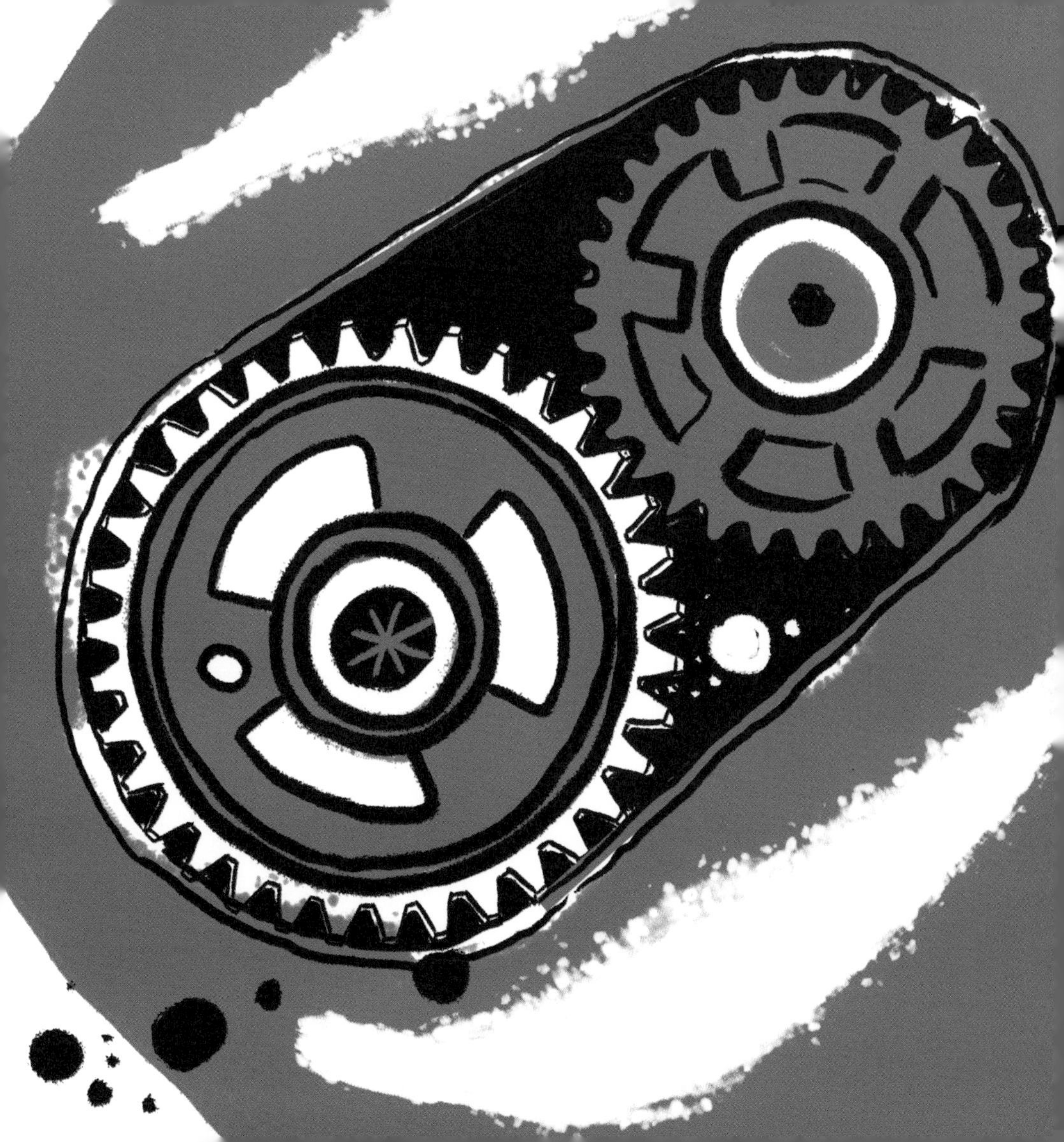

Do not pressure your child to agree to marry someone who appears suitable to you but not to them. It is for your child to decide whom they want to marry.

―❦

The decision to marry someone cannot emerge from depression and tears. On the contrary, it needs to be made with all your capacities and full peace of mind. Remember, you are not the only person to have experienced the cycle of doubt.

If the condition for marriage is that you make a dramatic change to your way of life – such as changing your profession – look for a more suitable spouse.

The first years of marriage, with their new obligations and expenses, are the most difficult. It would not be a good idea to add to these difficulties by beginning your new life in a country where you do not speak the language, and where the mentality is totally different.

Do not take rejection to heart. If it were destined to be a match, it would have materialized. Clearly it was not meant to be.

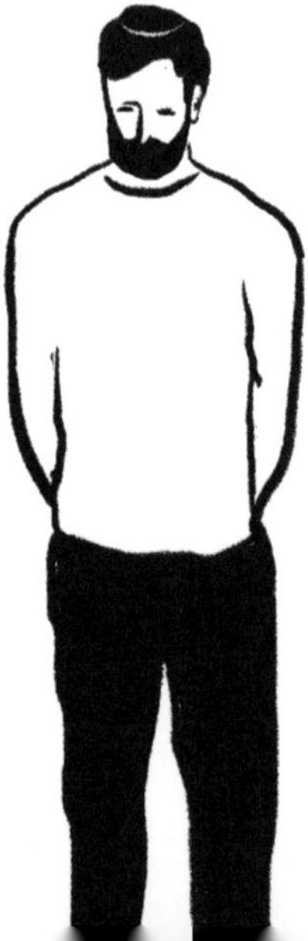

ADDENDUM II

WEDDING ANXIETY

YOUR CONTRIBUTION

Creating a dwelling place for G-d in this world necessitates spending money on holy acts. When an opportunity arises to spend even a small amount for a good purpose, do not let it pass you by. This applies to a wedding, too. Even if the other party offers to pay for everything, you should make a point of contributing something.

Marriage is an everlasting edifice, and the preparations for a wedding should be the same – stable and harmonious.

When the two sides' parents have disagreements about the details of their children's wedding, they should not involve the engaged couple.

If both the bride's and groom's families have agreed on critical details of the wedding ceremony, would it be wise to renegotiate them?

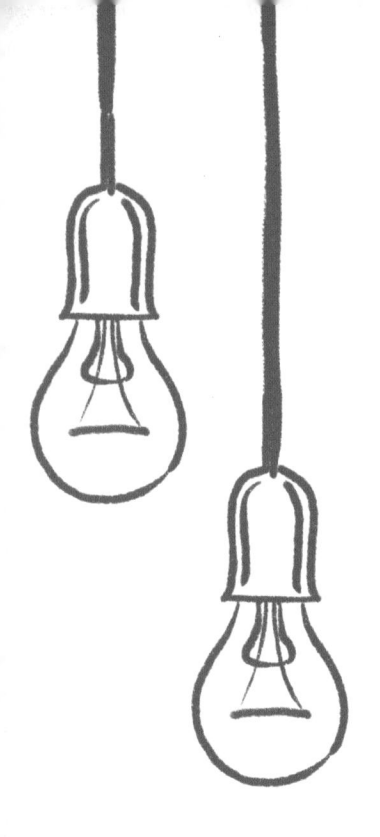

EXTRAVAGANT

A wedding should bring together many people without being materialistic or extravagant. When it comes to spiritual matters, however, no expense should be spared.

ADDENDUM III

BUILD MIKVAHS!

Mikvah Urgency

When a group of rabbinical students from Brooklyn visited Atlantic City, New Jersey, in 1963, the community expected to hear some inspirational lectures on Judaism, nothing more. But a simple request by the students on Shabbat morning started the community on a journey that led to the construction of the city's first mikvah.

Rabbi Aaron Kraus was a student at Yeshiva University when he agreed to host a class in Tanya, the fundamental text of Chabad philosophy, in his dorm room. A young Chabad rabbi, Berel Baumgarten, delivered the weekly Tuesday-night class to a group of students, and the two men became friends.

When he graduated, Rabbi Kraus took a position at a Conservative temple in Atlantic City and shortly thereafter invited Rabbi Baumgarten to lecture at the synagogue on a weekend. Rabbi Baumgarten arrived with three friends, among them a young man named Mottel Kalmanson, and all three addressed the community until late Friday night.

On Shabbat morning, the students asked where they could find a mikvah in order to immerse before prayers. The response: none existed in Atlantic City!

"Atlantic City was known to have a large Jewish population," remembered Rabbi Kalmanson. "We could not believe there was no mikvah there." Immediately after Shabbat, the students leaped into action and encouraged Rabbi Kraus to organize a meeting. A group gathered that night and a committee was established. "The young rabbis sparked our interest in having a mikvah," Rabbi Kraus said.

When the three men returned to New York, they wrote a report to the Rebbe detailing the events of the weekend. In response, the Rebbe's aide, Rabbi Mordechai Hodakov, requested on behalf of the Rebbe that Rabbi Kalmanson spearhead the mikvah-building project.

Rabbi Kalmanson returned frequently to Atlantic City, but progress on the mikvah was slow. "There were few experts and we needed funding," he recalled.

The Rebbe's dedication to the project never wavered. In a private audience with the Rebbe, when Rabbi Kalmanson expressed interest in getting married, the Rebbe responded, "Currently you're involved in one project [the mikvah], and when you finish that one, you can move on to the next!"

The committee purchased a property and began drafting a blueprint. The Rebbe arranged for Rabbi Nissan Telushkin, a renowned mikvah expert, to assist, and Rabbi Meir Greenberg, the chief rabbi of Patterson, New Jersey, also joined the effort.

In the early stages of the building process, Rabbi Kalmanson brought Mr. Irving Summers, a local businessman who was supporting the project, to a gathering with the Rebbe on the holiday of Purim. During a pause between talks, the two men approached the Rebbe, and Mr. Summers presented the Rebbe and Rabbi Kalmanson with wristwatches. The Rebbe agreed to accept the watch on condition that Mr. Summers accept the position of president of the Atlantic City mikvah. Summers obliged.

On another occasion, Rabbi Kalmanson brought a large group from the Atlantic City community to a gathering in 770, in hopes of cementing their commitment to building the mikvah. At the gathering, the Rebbe spoke at length about the importance of mikvahs. "The obligations to fulfill G-d's commandments and to learn Torah begin when a boy turns 13, or a girl turns 12. Yet there is one commandment in which a person participates even before conception: the commandment to be pure, to go to a mikvah, so that the birth should be sanctified," he said.

Nine months before a child is born, the Rebbe explained, a woman should lead a holy and healthy life, so that the infant be born with a healthy body and soul. "It is incumbent on the parents that they act in the proper way," the Rebbe said, "since their actions also affect the future child. Therefore, we understand the great reward that our sages tell us is given for fulfilling this mitzvah."

He concluded, "We might think that the building of a mikvah is the obligation of the rabbi, the ritual slaughterer, the teacher, or the synagogue's committee, while, in fact, it's everyone's obligation."

Despite the Rebbe's efforts, the project progressed very slowly, and later that year, during a private audience, the Rebbe told Rabbi Kalmanson that if the mikvah did not move forward, he would have to return the watch to Mr. Summers.

Mr. Summers took the message to heart and soon thereafter, in the summer of 1964, the community convened for the groundbreaking.

"Groundbreaking ceremonies for an ultramodern mikvah (ritualarium)," reported the *Atlantic City Press*, "will take place Sunday at 2 p.m. The structure will be the only one of its kind in Atlantic County."

The newspaper explained that, "A mikvah is defined as a ritual bath, built according to rabbinic specifications. . . . The primary goal

[is] family purity, a tradition that has been kept alive even under the most adverse conditions in Jewish history." The newspaper noted the Rebbe's involvement in "making this sacred project a reality."

The Rebbe sent Chabad luminaries Rabbi Yochonon Gordon and Rabbi Zalman Duchman to represent him at the groundbreaking.

In a letter addressed to the gathered crowd, the Rebbe made clear what he expected from the event:

> *It is gratifying indeed that the efforts of your society, under rabbinic leadership headed by Rabbi Moshe Shapiro [the chief rabbi of Atlantic City], have reached this milestone. With all of you, I hope and pray that the construction of the mikvah will proceed with all speed, so that it will soon be possible to joyously celebrate the completion of the mikvah with blessing and gratitude to the Almighty.*

The Rebbe added:

> *We all know well the importance of* zerizut *[swiftness] in the fulfillment of all mitzvot [Jewish observances]. ... It is obvious how very important it is to follow through with the utmost* zerizut *such a great and comprehensive mitzvah as [building] a mikvah, which is one of the foundations of the House of Israel and one of the main pillars of every Jewish community.*

Yet progress on the building

was slow due to the daunting cost. During this time, the synagogue of Rabbi Greenberg, who had been involved in the mikvah committee, was vandalized.

Rabbi Greenberg informed the Rebbe of this devastating event, and the Rebbe's response was that the time to complete the mikvah project in Atlantic City had arrived. Rabbi Greenberg devoted himself anew, and soon the mikvah was completed, to the delight of the entire community. Dedicated members of the Jewish community maintained the mikvah for many years. However, the neighborhood declined, the mikvah piping was vandalized, and the building was later condemned by the city. In 1983, when Rabbi Shmuel Rapoport arrived in Atlantic City as a Chabad emissary, he immediately focused on building a new mikvah.

Call Back!

One day in 1971, the director of the Hebrew Academy in Long Beach, California, Rabbi Gershon Schusterman, received a call at the office from Rabbi Binyomin Klein, one of the Rebbe's aides. He was calling with a message from the Rebbe, which he said was in response to a letter.

"I didn't ask anything from the Rebbe," Rabbi Schusterman answered in bewilderment. "Are you sure it is for me?"

Rabbi Klein assured him that it was and relayed the Rebbe's message: "The idea to build a mikvah in Long Beach is extremely important, and in order to speed up the process, I am sending a check for $1,000 by special delivery."

Rabbi Schusterman hung up and immediately contacted the other Chabad representatives in the area, but none of them had written to the Rebbe about a mikvah.

The next day, Rabbi Klein called the Chabad House office again, explaining that the Rebbe had advised him to speak to one of the rebbetzins about building the mikvah.

Rabbi Mendel Futerfas, a man of self-sacrifice who spent years in prison for his activities on behalf of Jewish life in the Soviet Union, would travel to Long Beach every year for a Hasidic gathering, where he would give advice and encouragement to the community. Realizing that there was no mikvah in Long Beach, Rabbi Futerfas had encouraged the crowd at that year's gathering to build one.

It turned out that one of the women present had written a letter to her mother describing the gathering. Her mother, Miriam Popack, a member of the executive committee of the Lubavitch Women's Organization, presented the letter to the Rebbe. The Rebbe immediately asked his aide to convey his response.

The incident inspired the community to build a beautiful mikvah.

From Kabul to Bangkok

Young and energetic, Rabbi Shmuel Bogomilsky was always ready for an adventure. Like many other Chabad rabbinical students, he spent the summer months traveling to locations across the globe to help Jewish communities in need of material and spiritual assistance.

In the summer of 1963, Rabbi Bogomilsky visited more than ten communities across Asia and Europe, eventually making his way to Kabul, Afghanistan. He carried with him a recommendation from Mayer and Yehuda Abraham, Afghani gem dealers in New York whom he met through his travel agent.

In the Kabul airport, Rabbi Bogomilsky noticed that an American man was watching him closely. The man approached and introduced himself as a member of the United States Peace Corps stationed in the country. It turned out that he was Jewish and had a working relationship with the local Jewish community. He arranged for the rabbi to meet one of the community leaders: Aron Aranoff.

Mr. Aranoff was wary at first, wondering what this young man from Brooklyn wanted from him and the community. But he soon recognized that the rabbi was there only to help. That night a meeting was called, and Rabbi Bogomilsky introduced himself.

The community's situation was dire. Only a remnant remained of the original 500 families, the vast majority having moved to Israel after the War of

Independence in 1948. By the time the rabbi arrived, there was no synagogue building and suitable mikvah. The last few Jewish families were forced to share homes with Muslims. Prayer services were held quietly in private apartments.

The community was in a slumber, and Rabbi Bogomilsky wanted to revive it. During his short visit he began to lobby the community about the importance of having a synagogue building and a mikvah. He organized the funds necessary to begin building and encouraged community leaders to seek permits.

Back in New York, he continued his efforts. He wrote letters prompting the community to move ahead with the building. The construction of the mikvah, a complicated process usually overseen by a rabbi, would prove the most challenging part of the project.

Rabbi Bogomilsky wrote a detailed plan and had an artist create a rendering of the mikvah. The Rebbe took great interest in this project and reviewed the plans to make sure that the minute details would be understood. Among many other suggestions, the Rebbe stressed that the measurements should be precise, reminding Rabbi Bogomilsky to take into account the thickness of the tiles when giving the dimensions for the pit.

The community in Kabul raised half of the needed funds, and they asked for Rabbi Bogomilsky's help in raising the remaining $10,000. Rabbi Bogomilsky approached Mayer and Yehuda Abraham, who had introduced him to his Afghani friends. He also arranged for them, and the Afghani community, to visit the Rebbe.

The Rebbe spoke to the gem dealers about the importance of a mikvah and offered to give $4,000 toward the project himself. The men said that they would fund it, accepting only a nominal contribution from the Rebbe.

When the community began to dig the pit for the mikvah, they found an underground well. They used this natural water source for the mikvah, the preferred construction. The remaining Afghani Jews used the mikvah and synagogue for many years. Today, there is only one Jew left in Kabul, who cares for the synagogue.

The Abrahams stayed in contact with the Rebbe. The headquarters of their gem dealership were in New York, but they had offices in several countries, including one in Bangkok, Thailand, and at one point Mr. Mayer Abraham was spending much of his time there.

Hearing of this, the Rebbe encouraged him to build a mikvah in Bangkok. The Rebbe wrote:

> *There is surely no need to emphasize to you at length the great importance of a mikvah, which is one of the essential, divinely given observances, which has an impact not only on persons observing it, but also on their children and children's children, to the end of posterity. It is also a mitzvah which hastens the the complete redemption, which is connected with purity, as it is written, "I shall sprinkle upon you pure water, and you shall be pure" (Ezekiel 36:25).*

The Bangkok community was small. Perhaps only two or three women would ever use the mikvah, yet the Rebbe felt that it was important to build one, even for so few. Mr. Abraham, always open to new challenges and passionate about Jewish causes, shared the Rebbe's enthusiasm for the project.

Building a mikvah in Bangkok was not going to be easy, however. Sometimes called the Venice of the East, the city is built above canals, which makes digging deep into the ground difficult. The mikvah would need to have a unique design, where the pool would be aboveground.

When Rabbi Shalom Ber Hecht took charge of the synagogue where Mr. Mayer Abraham was a member, his visits to the Rebbe became more frequent.

One year in the late 1970s, the Abrahams and members of the Afghani Jewish community brought the Rebbe a birthday gift of precious historical documents. When Mr. Abraham made a toast, the Rebbe told him that the best birthday gift would be the mikvah in Bangkok.

The Abrahams promised that they would build it, but the project lagged. Despite the many challenges involved, the Rebbe never gave up. Every time Mr. Abraham visited, the Rebbe would ask him, "What is with the mikvah in Bangkok?"

It took some ten years until the mikvah was completed in the 1980s. Shortly thereafter, Chabad representatives moved to the city. Today, the mikvah is used by many more than the two or three that it was built for.

A Communal Mikvah

When Rabbi Israel Haber accepted a job as a chaplain at the Elmendorf Air Force Base in Anchorage, Alaska, in 1973, he immediately began to worry about how his wife would manage without a mikvah.

On their way to Alaska, the Habers stopped in St. Paul, Minnesota, and spent Shabbat at the Chabad house there. Rabbi Haber raised the burning issue of the mikvah with the rabbi. "Don't worry," the rabbi told him. "If you get the permits, we will do everything else to build the mikvah."

At first the Habers thought it would be easy for Mrs. Haber to travel to the mikvah in Seattle every month. But one flight in the belly of a Lockheed C-130H convinced them that it was not a good plan.

Rabbi Haber began to take the idea of building a mikvah on the base seriously. He got clearance from the Air Force and a budget for the building materials. When the plans were in place, Rabbi Gershon Grossbaum, a Chabad rabbi from Minnesota, came to oversee the building of the primitive but kosher mikvah for the chaplain's wife to use once a month.

Rabbi Grossbaum informed the Rebbe about the project, and the Rebbe sent a warm letter to Rabbi Haber telling him that he had the great merit to build the first mikvah in Anchorage "for the Alaskan Jewish community."

In his two-page letter, the Rebbe

wrote that the chaplain surely knew the great importance of the mikvah; however, as our sages say, one should "encourage the energetic":

> *I wish to express my confident hope that you are doing all you can to make the mikvah a busy place, frequented regularly, not only by the women who directly benefit from your good influence, but also by their friends and acquaintances who will be induced by them to follow their example. And while this kind of religious inspiration is a "must" wherever Jews live, it is even more so in the city and state where the mikvah has just been established for the first time.*

Later, at an audience in New York, the Rebbe advised Mrs. Haber to gather all of the elderly Jewish women in Anchorage and encourage them to go to the mikvah. As the Rebbe often explained:

> *A special effort should be made to influence women who have reached the age of menopause, the so-called "change of life." It should be explained to them that by proper preparation and going to the mikvah this one time. . . . It would purify them for the rest of their lives.*

The Rebbe then blessed the Habers, who at the time did not have children, that they should have many children who would become great rabbis and educators.

The couple left Alaska three years

later in 1976 and moved to California. In 1980, before traveling to Israel, the Habers had a private audience with the Rebbe. The Rebbe inquired about their young child, about the community in Alaska, and especially about the mikvah.

The Rebbe told Rabbi Haber that he should fly back to Alaska to check on the mikvah and "to fix anything that needs to be corrected."

Rabbi Haber asked how long he should stay there, and the Rebbe said a short visit would be fine. Rabbi Haber flew to Alaska on Friday, checked that the mikvah was still kosher and in use, and returned to Israel on Sunday.

When permanent Chabad representatives arrived in Alaska in 1991, they used the mikvah and encouraged others to do the same.

In 1999, the Air Force informed the Chabad representatives in Anchorage that the mikvah was going to be demolished. A fund was established for a new mikvah, which was built and is still in use today.

Is It Warm?

During the 1982 Lebanon War, Chabad representatives arrived in Bhamdoun, Lebanon, a small town some 15 miles from Beirut, with a "mitzvah tank," a mobile home equipped with all the supplies necessary for Jewish observance. They were there to lift the spirits of the IDF, so they were surprised when a local Jew approached them.

The Jew told them that the synagogue in the town had been taken over by terrorists. Though the terrorists were now gone, bombing had badly damaged the mikvah, making it unusable. The Chabad rabbis promised to help, and by the next Sunday they were on their way back to Bhamdoun with building materials to repair the mikvah.

The renovations were completed, the mikvah was now kosher, and the rabbis went home. Rabbi Levi Bistritzky, who oversaw the project, wrote about it to the Rebbe. The Rebbe responded, "Is there a heater that warms the water in the mikvah?"

Not content that the Jews in this small Lebanese town had a kosher mikvah, the Rebbe wanted to ensure that using it would be a pleasant experience. Rabbi Bistritzky immediately got to work and had an electric water heater installed.

ATTRACTIVE

Every effort should be made to encourage women to go to the mikvah. Thus, it is important to beautify the physical building, the amenities, and the furnishings.

Have a charity box at the mikvah, so one could
drop a few coins in the box before immersing.

A mikvah should never be shuttered.
When a new one is built, the upkeep of the
old should be scrupulously continued.

Encourage more women to come. When more
people use the mikvah, the costs go down. Of course,
the savings should be passed on to the mikvah
attendees, and thus the fees should be lowered.

Sources

Adapted freely from the correspondence, talks and audiences of the Lubavitcher Rebbe. Below are the dates and sources (note that several of the quotes are not published and are therefore not sourced to any specific volume):

Page 12 **Atomic Energy** Private audience, early 1960s.

Page 14 **Dating for Fun** From an audience with teens, 1963.

Page 15 **Toxic Love** Letter, 1976.

Page 16 **Equation of Two** Undated response (*Petakim* 1:154).

Page 25 **Three Circles** Talk at a wedding, September 12, 1951 (*Torat Menachem* 3:293).

Page 26 **Ring Giving** Talks, February 25, 1989 (*Lekutei Sichot* 39:34) and September 11, 1954 (*Lekutei Sichot* 19:218).

Page 27 **Monetary Reminder** Talk, September 11, 1954 (*Lekutei Sichot* 19: 220).

Page 30 **The Edifice** Letter, 1970 (*Memento*, October 20, 2013, P. 2).

Page 34 **Reciprocity Effect** Talks, July 16, 1984 (*Torat Menachem 5744,* 4:2242) and April 23, 1990 (*Torat Menachem 5750* 3:113).

Page 36 **Blessings Explained** Notes for a speech in 1944 (*Reshimot* 1:21).

Page 39 **Dance!** Discourse, February 2, 1955 (*Torat Menachem* 13:206).

Page 44 **The Goal** Talk, November 25, 1989 (*Torat Menachem 5750*,

1:376).

Page 45 **Seeing the Unity** Talk, October 6, 1970 (*Lekutei Sichot* 17:175).

Page 48 **Gift Not Wanted?** Letter, March 1, 1976 (*Igrot Kodesh* 31:144).

Page 56 **Finding Good** Letters, October 9, 1942 (*Igrot Kodesh* 1:48) and March 26, 1944 (*Igrot Kodesh* 1:275).

Page 57 **Full Personhood** Undated notes of a 1940s talk (*Reshimot* 5:45).

Page 58 **Wedding Never Ends** Compiled from several talks (*Shaarei Nisu'in,* p. 190).

Page 63 Talk, May 21, 1983 (*Torat Menachem 5743*, 3:1610).

Page 64 Letter, 1974 (*Memento*, October 20, 2013, Page 55); Undated response, (*Petakim* 2:167); Letter from September 15, 1959 (*Igrot Kodesh* 18:525).

Page 65 Undated response (*Petakim* 1:173); Letter, 1970 (*Memento*, October 20, 2013, Page 50); Letter, 1972 (*Memento*, ibid., pp. 44-5).

Page 66 Letters, 1972 and 1977 (*Memento*, ibid., pp. 8 & 13; *Petakim* 1:148).

Page 67 Letters, 1970 and 1974 (*Memento*, ibid., pp. 50 & 54).

Page 70 **Perfection** Letter, 1973 (Memento, ibid., Page 47).

Page 71 **Relative Perfection** Letter, 1966 (*Memento*, ibid., pp. 56-57).

Page 72 Undated response (*Petakim* 1:180); Letter, 1970 (*Memento*, ibid., Page 50); Letters, 1975 & 1970 (*Memento*, ibid., pp. 42 & 51).

Page 73 Undated response, (*Petakim*

2:177); Undated response (*Petakim* 1:182).

Page 76 Undated response (*Memento*, December 1, 2016, Page 10).

Page 84 **All-Encompassing** *Sefer Halikutim*, the letter Mem, Page 557.

Page 85 **Total Immersion** Talk, October 18, 1952 (*Lekutei Sichot*, 1:4–5).

Page 86 **Stepping Stones** Talks, June 27, 1964 and January 15, 1966 (*Lekutei Sichot*, 6:25ff).

Page 88 *Sefer Halikutim*, Nun, Page 39ff; Notes, 1933 (*Reshimot*, 1:345ff); ibid., pp. 344ff.

Page 89 Talk, December 5, 1963 (*Lekutei Sichot* 14:26ff); Letter, January 15, 1952 (*Igrot Kodesh*, 5:144).

Page 92 **Protective Garments** Talk, June 24, 1975 (*Lekutei Sichot* 13:260ff).

Page 94 **Greater Heights** *Torat Shalom 5766,* pp. 11ff.

Page 95 **The Outcome** Talk, November 6, 1956 (*Lekutei Sichot* 1:14).

Page 97 **Humility** *Sefer Halikutim*, the letter Mem, Page 561.

Page 98 *Igrot Kodesh Rayatz*, 4:165, *Torat Shalom – Sefer Hasichot,* Page 165, *Torat Menachem 5715,* Page 163, *Lekutei Sichot* 8:72ff. and Lekutei Torah 43:3.

Page 102 **The Search** Letter, January 14, 1955 (*Igrot Kodesh* 10:249ff).

Page 103 **Your Effort** Letter, February 13, 1947 (*Igrot Kodesh* 2:195).

Page 106 Letters, March 23, 1954 (*Igrot Kodesh* 8:285, *Neilchah Be'Orchotav* 166) and November 24, 1955 (*Igrot Kodesh* 12:130); Letter, January 19, 1955 (*Memento,* October 9, 2013, Page 19); Letters, February 20, 1958 (*Igrot Kodesh* 16:306) and August 6, 1959 (*Igrot Kodesh*

Page 110 Undated letter *(Petakim* 1:147).

Page 112 Letter, 1972 *(Memento,* ibid., Page 7).

Page 114 Letter, February 4, 1974 *(Igrot Kodesh* 29:85); Letter, January 1, 1957 *(Igrot Kodesh* 14:316); Undated response *(Shidduchin Venisuin* 2:314).

Page 115 Letter, September 30, 1957 *(Memento,* November 12, 2017, Page 5); Letter, October 28, 1954 *(Memento,* October 9, 2013, Page 18); 18:280).

Page 118 **Your Contribution** Private audience, 1960s *(Simchat Olam,* pp. 110ff; see *Lekutei Sichot,* pp. 5:80ff).

Page 119 Letter, December 1965 *(Choveret Hitvaadut,* Vayishlach 5774).

Page 120 Extravagant Private audience, 1960s *(Simchat Olam,* p. 107ff).

Page 138 Letter, January 9, 1955 *(Igrot Kodesh,* 10:227; *Shaarei Halacha Uminhag,* 3:116).

Page 139 Conversation, June 10, 1990; Letter, August 28, 1952 *(Igrot Kodesh,* 6:319); Letter, June 21, 1955 *(Igrot Kodesh,* 11:207).

Acknowledgements

It was a daunting task to once again dig through the hundreds of volumes of the Rebbe's teachings and sort out guidance that could be categorized as practical advice. I'm grateful to all those who assisted, and in some cases took the lead, in making the Rebbe's words accessible to a wider audience.

This project was made possible by my wife, Chana Raizel, who for several years now has been nudging and cajoling behind the scenes for a new edition of the book. She arranged the funding and found the artist — this book is truly to her credit.

My thanks to Miriam Goldshmid, who with her husband, Nochi, dedicated this book in loving memory of her mother, Baila Friedman, of blessed memory.

The *Advice for Life* series was initiated by the unforgettable Rabbi Simcha Zirkind, of blessed memory. It was his dream to bring the Rebbe's message to every person. Surely he would be gratified to know that the series has currently printed over a half-million copies on a variety of subjects. This book was subsidized by his organization, Ezrat Israel, headed by his wife, Frieda, and children.

"Living Waters" was originally created for the opening of the Mei Chaya Mushka Mikvah in 2016. My thanks to the unstoppable Moshe

Pinson, who spearheaded that project and has played an active role in many other projects of the Hasidic Archives.

To my children, Motti, Meir, Shaina, Benny and Mendel, who are always there to brighten my day, I give my deep appreciation.

The editor, Sarah Ogince, has done a superb job in making this book what it is. Her questions, comments, and critique brought the clarity to the text that I had envisioned.

A new addition to the energetic team at Hasidic Archives, Annita Soble contributed the thought-provoking illustrations and brought the Rebbe's ideas to life.

With appreciation to Mushka Kanner for the superb design and layout.

I thank all those who opened their hearts to tell me the stories included in this book.

Rabbi Aaron Raskin reviewed the material for accuracy, and Yerachmiel Glassner, Alex Heppenheimer, Rabbi Avraham Kievman, Mimi Palace, Chana Sharfstein, and Rabbi Moshe Zaklikofsky assisted with copy editing and fact checking.

Thank you to Rabbis Chaim Shaul Bruk, Mordechai Laufer, Shalom Dovber Levine, Chaim Rapaport, and Michoel Aron Seligson, from whose publications and indices some of the material was derived.

"Praise to G-d, for He is good, for His kindness is everlasting!"

Dovid

IN LOVING MEMORY OF
Baila Friedman

To the many who unburdened themselves to her, Baila Friedman was more than simply a listening ear. She was a dear friend who made the effort to put herself in their shoes and tailor her responses to their needs. Her advice was practical, personal, and wise — she never lost sight of the bigger picture.

Whether you called her late at night, dropped by for an afternoon visit, or bumped into her at the supermarket, when you talked to Baila, you were the only person who existed, and she had known you all your life.

As a teacher of soon-to-be-married brides, she forged relationships that lasted for years after the weddings, as the young women turned to her again and again for guidance. More powerful than her words was the example she set, the way she conducted her home with respect and joy.

Her door was always open, and the needy were welcomed in with a smile, a bowl of hot soup, and a charitable gift. "Life is in G-d's hands," she would say. "We need to make the best of it."

Her children and grandchildren carry on her legacy of kindness and good deeds.

DEDICATED TO

Rabbi Simcha Zirkind

who lovingly dedicated his life, as a Chabad representative, to the Jewish communities in Tunisia, Canada, and beyond.

DEDICATED TO

our children and grandchildren

שיחיו

By Rabbi **Zushe** and **Esther Wilhelm**

They should be blessed materially and spiritually with all of their hearts' desires and much nachas *from their children and grandchildren.*

~≈

In the merit of emissaries of the Rebbe
to Ft. Lauderdale, Florida,

Rabbi **Moishe Meir** and **Penina Lipszyc**

and their children,

Menachem Mendel, **Yacha Golda**, **Gitty**, **Levi Yitzchok and Devorah Leah**,

for success in all their material and spiritual endeavors

DEDICATED TO

Rebbetzin Esther Bukiet

of blessed memory

By her children and grandchildren

Zaklikowski family

Hollywood, Florida

Smetana family

Brooklyn, New York

Zaklikowski family

Brooklyn, New York

More from the Advice for Life series

Learning on the Job
Jewish Career Lessons

Kaleidoscope
Uplifting Views on Daily Life

Daily Life

From Life to Life

Dignified Differences
A Special Soul

Hasidic Archives books are available at special discounts for bulk purchases in the United States for corporations, institutions, and other organizations. For more information, please contact us at HasidicArchives@Gmail.com.